T0299223

ROUTLEDGE LIBRARY EDITIONS:
EMPLOYEE OWNERSHIP AND
ECONOMIC DEMOCRACY

Volume 9

THE ORIGINS OF ECONOMIC DEMOCRACY

THE ORIGINS OF
ECONOMIC DEMOCRACY

Profit-sharing and employee-shareholding schemes

MICHAEL POOLE

Routledge
Taylor & Francis Group

LONDON AND NEW YORK

First published in 1989 by Routledge

This edition first published in 2018
by Routledge
2 Park Square, Milton Park, Abingdon, Oxon OX14 4RN

and by Routledge
605 Third Avenue, New York, NY 10017

Routledge is an imprint of the Taylor & Francis Group, an informa business

British Library Cataloguing in Publication Data
A catalogue record for this book is available from the British Library

ISBN: 978-1-138-29962-7 (Set)
ISBN: 978-1-315-12163-5 (Set) (ebk)
ISBN: 978-1-138-30787-2 (Volume 9) (hbk)
ISBN: 978-1-315-14263-0 (Volume 9) (ebk)

Publisher's Note
The publisher has gone to great lengths to ensure the quality of this reprint but points out that some imperfections in the original copies may be apparent.

Disclaimer
The publisher has made every effort to trace copyright holders and would welcome correspondence from those they have been unable to trace.

THE ORIGINS
OF ECONOMIC
DEMOCRACY

Profit~sharing and
employee~shareholding
schemes

Michael Poole

Routledge
London and New York

First published 1989 by Routledge
11 New Fetter Lane, London EC4P 4EE
29 West 35th Street, New York, NY 10001

© 1989 Michael Poole

Printed in Great Britain by
Billing & Sons Ltd, Worcester

British Library Cataloguing in Publication Data

Poole, Michael, *1943–*
    The origins of economic democracy : profit-
    sharing and employee-shareholding schemes.
    1. Great Britain. Profit sharing
    I. Title
    331.2'164

    ISBN 0–415–02555–9

Library of Congress Cataloging in Publication Data

Poole, Michael.
    The origins of economic democracy.
    Profit-sharing and employee-shareholding schemes
    Bibliography: v. 1, p.
    Includes index.
    1. Profit-sharing——Great Britain.   2. Employee
stock options——Great Britain.   I. Title.
HD3025.A4P66   1989   331.2'164   88–30663
ISBN 0–415–02555–9 (v.1)

Contents

Figures

Tables

Tables

Preface

This study is concerned with a detailed examination of profit-sharing and employee-shareholding schemes with special reference to the British experience. The issues raised and the data presented are set out in two interrelated volumes. The first involves an account of the origins and development of schemes, while the second entails an assessment of their consequences for the economic and industrial relations performance of companies, the degree of satisfaction of employees, and the extent to which the introduction of profit sharing and other related practices has occasioned changes in work practices and organizational flexibility.

The data presented in the two monographs derive from a project initiated in the Social Science Branch of the Department of Employment and sponsored by this particular governmental department. The early design work was undertaken by Gillian Smith, who subsequently produced an article from the survey stage of the research entitled 'Profit sharing and employee share ownership in Britain' for the *Employment Gazette* (September 1986, pp. 380–5). There were two principal phases to the project: (1) a survey of companies in Britain; and (2) case studies of selected firms derived from the enterprises included in stage one.

The survey commenced with a series of short telephone screening interviews in 1,125 companies that were designed to obtain information on the extent of profit-sharing and employee-shareholding schemes in Britain and to provide a sample for subsequent detailed interviews. This was followed by the so-called 'main-stage' survey of 303 firms in Britain in which a wide range of data were gathered on the operation of schemes and the factors associated with their adoption or non-adoption. The questionnaires for the survey were developed jointly by IFF Research Limited, Social Science Branch of the Department of Employment, and Michael Poole. The fieldwork was carried out in May 1985 by IFF under the direction of Judy Morrell. In August 1985, a data tape was transferred to the University of Wales Institute of Science and Technology to enable Michael Poole to conduct a more detailed analysis of the survey material. At this point, Joan Wright carried out the necessary computing work with considerable speed and skill.

At the design stage of the research, it was recognized that a further case-study phase would be necessary in order to allow for a detailed exploration of the specific processes which lead companies to introduce profit sharing and the problems encountered developing schemes. Above all, it was considered important that an assessment should be made of the views of employees. In consequence, the Department of Employment commissioned Michael Poole to carry out the case-study phase, which included: (1) detailed interviews with key management respondents; (2) interviews with full-time trade union officers and lay representatives; (3) the gathering of data on company performance; and (4) the administering of a questionnaire to a substantial number of employees (approximately 2,000).

The case-study phase of the research commenced in Spring 1986 and involved twenty-two companies selected from the 303 firms in the 'main-stage' survey. To ensure a regional balance, the companies were divided equally between South Wales/the south-west of England and London/the south-east of England (further details and a justification for the methods used will appear in the second volume). The case-study phase was directed by Michael Poole, while Glenville Jenkins and Michael Gasiorek provided research assistance. The particularly valuable role of Glenville Jenkins in the research is reflected in the joint authorship of the second volume.

During the survey stage of the research Francis Butler was integrally involved in the project and Peter Brannen chaired various meetings of both the survey and case-study phases. Towards the end of the case studies, Neil Millward assumed chairmanship of the steering committee meetings. At UWIST, Brian Moores and Andy Thompson provided valuable advice on statistical techniques for handling the survey data.

Throughout the survey and case-study stages, Gillian Smith handled the project with considerable skill and thoroughness. Valuable comments were provided by members of the steering committee for the case studies and especially by Stephen Creigh, John Cullinane, Dorothy Green, and Michael Lott. In the case-study companies, there were many respondents who gave considerably of their knowledge and time and, without such assistance, the project could not have been a success. The comments of Euan

Cameron were particularly insightful in this respect. Richard Long helped considerably by providing a copy of a questionnaire from his own research which helped to inform many of the items in the employee-attitudes survey. IFF Research, and especially Judy Morrell, offered very valuable assistance to the UWIST research team to secure contacts with the case-study companies. Moreover, for their considerable efforts in typing this monograph a special word of thanks is due to Sally Jarratt and Marina Miller.

It is hoped that the two volumes of this study will help to shed considerable light on the operation of profit-sharing and share-ownership schemes in Britain. The Department of Employment deserves particular gratitude for funding the research though, naturally, any views expressed are those of the author and do not necessarily reflect those of the funding body.

Michael Poole
Cardiff Business School

Chapter one

Introduction

The rise of profit-sharing and employee-shareholding schemes in the late twentieth century has been a phenomenon of considerable moment. Over the generations, financial participation has of course been comprehended as elemental to a property-owning democracy. This is a type of society involving a permanent change in the status of wage or salary earners to become partners in the firms in which they are employed. Moreover, it is a type of social and industrial organization which has been seen to eradicate the excessive concentration of wealth and share capital and, in the long term, to bring in its train the erosion of political philosophies aimed at destroying the capitalist system itself (Copeman *et al.* 1984: 15).

But notwithstanding the importance of the modern expansion of employee financial participation, is it realistic to expect such fundamental changes in the status of working people and in their political philosophies arising from the introduction of profit sharing and employee share ownership? Why has the growth of these schemes been experienced in several (but not all) advanced industrial economies at a similar period in time? What is the current extent of employee shareholding in Britain and why do some firms adopt schemes whereas other companies have so far failed to develop them?

The aim of this study is to attempt to provide answers to these and other fundamental questions. To this end, a conceptual clarification of the main themes is first undertaken. This is followed by a brief account of the history of profit sharing in Britain and a review of current experiences in a number of advanced and developing countries. Various theoretical models are then elucidated with attention focusing on five main sets of explanatory conditions which are assessed empirically. These are: (1) the role of government and the legislature; (2) economic 'infrastructural' conditions; (3) managerial strategic choices; (4)

1

industrial relations climate within the firm; and (5) the power and
strategies of other organized groups in the company.

Economic and industrial democracy

Although this study is primarily concerned with profit-sharing and
employee-shareholding schemes, it is important at the outset to
attempt a conceptual clarification of the main issues involved. A
basic distinction between economic and industrial democracy is
first drawn. These conceptions are then synthesized in an inclusive
theory of organizational democracy.

For the purposes of definition, the term economic democracy is
typically used to denote a variety of forms of employee participation in the ownership of enterprises and in the distribution of
economic rewards. By contrast, industrial democracy refers to the
notion of worker participation in decision making and employee
involvement in the processes of control within the firm.

In figure 1.1, these distinctions are elucidated, with the two axes
representing different types of economic and industrial democracy
respectively. The vertical axis indicates a variety of forms of
participation in ownership ranging from managerial equity and
executive profit-sharing schemes; through worker equity and all-
employee profit sharing; to capital sharing and to 'pure' economic
democracy based on the ownership of the enterprise by all its
members. The horizontal axis covers the classical and managerial
firms and then some of the many forms of industrial democracy
including works councils, worker board representation, and self-
management (for a review of types, see Poole 1986b).

The theory of organizational democracy: the favourable conjunctures thesis

Nevertheless, even though it is conceptually valuable to distinguish
between economic and industrial democracy, there are manifold
interconnections between them. This is not only because ownership has frequently been seen as the principal key to control the
organization of production and the division of labour (Ramsay and
Haworth 1984), but also because of the empirical probability that
the two forms of workplace democracy may advance in parallel.
*As a consequence, inclusive theories of organizational democracy
that encompass both participation in ownership and in decision
making within the firm have to be constructed.*

The theory of organizational democracy advanced here is based
on the notion of 'favourable conjunctures'. This approach involves

Figure 1.1 Degree of participation in control by members of a firm

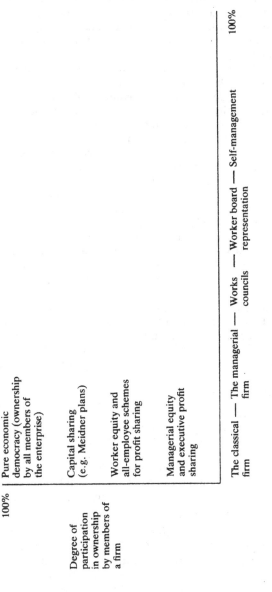

Source: Based on Abell (1985: 51).

Note: The vertical axis has been altered from the original to include capital sharing, all-employee profit sharing, and executive profit-sharing schemes.

the isolation of *underlying* factors which account for the rise of economic and industrial democracy; but it does not assume the *inevitability* of either so-called evolutionary or cyclical movements in their development. To be sure, the 'favourable conjunctures' thesis does recognize a broad long-term trend towards organizational democracy; but it identifies a discontinuous historical pattern within this very general tendency. It encompasses various comparative theories and the possibility of spatial and temporal differences within any given society. It infers that given institutional forms of organizational democracy may be different at distinctive periods in time. And it recognizes that *some* forms of organizational democracy develop on a 'counter-cyclical' basis.

It is important at the outset to argue that the 'favourable conjunctures' thesis is preferred here to the earlier evolutionary and cyclical approaches which have been the dominant interpretations of the rise of organizational democracy. Members of the 'evolutionary school' have characteristically argued that workplace democracy gradually unfolds alongside changes in the economic, political, and social fabric of advanced industrial societies. The earliest proponents of this position were avowedly Utopian. Indeed, even before the nineteenth century, it was possible to detect in the writings of Rousseau (1968) and Jefferson (see Beloff 1948) the advocacy of independent 'worker proprietors' as the essential foundation of just and equitable societies. Later, Mill envisaged economic and industrial democracy as a vehicle for self-development and the advancement of community. For him, the interlinking of 'productive' and 'consumptive' aspects of human activity through 'co-operatives' would occasion a 'moral revolution to society' and result in (Mill 1965: 792):

> the healing of the standing feud between capital and labour; the transformation of human life, from a conflict of classes struggling for opposite interests, to a friendly rivalry in the pursuit of a good common to all; the elevation of the dignity of labour; a new sense of security and independence in the labouring class; and the conversion of each human being's daily occupation into a school of social sympathies and practical intelligence.

Utopianism continued to characterize debates in the 1960s on this subject (see Pateman 1968). But gradually the evolutionary position became synonymous with the isolation of a series of favourable long-term movements that were understood to encourage a broadly linear advance of organizational democracy. The principal forces isolated included: the involvement of the state and the legislature in industrial relations; the growing concentration of industry and increased technical complexity of modern productive processes; the rise of the new managerial elite; a more educated and aspirant workforce with a more secure institutional base; and a gradual change in values of all groups in industry as the 'democratic current' was becoming increasingly ascendant.

In brief, then, evolutionary thinkers have argued that the state and the legislature have increasingly influenced moves towards organizational democracy. In their view, this has arisen partly because of a determination to regulate industrial relations, but also because of the electoral consequences of governments failing to secure labour peace by means of the active participation of the workforce in ownership and control of the enterprise. Moreover, the growing concentration of industry has been seen to enhance such a tendency because of the managerial problems involved in large-scale organization, a situation occasioned not least by the influence of trade unions in many publicly quoted companies. New technologies, too, require highly educated and proficient employees who will not accept without demur traditional modes of decision making in the firm. Modern managers are also likely to be well versed in those 'human-resourcing' techniques that promote employee involvement. Finally, changes in values (encapsulated in the notion of a 'democratic current' (Webb and Webb 1897)) have been viewed as broadly interconnected with the advance of organizational democracy.

The 'cyclical' approach

But by the early 1980s, a cyclical interpretation of organizational democracy had gained increasing currency in academic and popular debate. On this view, the idea that there are long-term movements in modern societies which consistently favour the advance of organizational democracy is disputed. Rather, the historical record is seen to comprise advances followed by later decay and even the abandonment of previously flourishing experiments (see Ramsay 1977, 1983).

It is basic to 'cyclical' theories, then, that periods of crisis (such as wartime or post-war reconstruction) or of domestic economic and industrial upheavals are favourable to organizational democracy. Certainly this was true of the two world wars and also of the periods of radical ferment in the early 1910s and 1920s and in the late 1960s and early 1970s. Social and political values have also varied appreciably over time, with the eras of experimentation in participation corresponding with the growth of democratic and egalitarian ideologies and a challenge to the decision-making prerogatives of management. Indeed, advances have typically seen to be in conditions in which in the immortal words of Flanders (1970: 172) managements are only able to 'regain control by sharing it'.

On such assumptions, the circumstances of the 1980s have not been as favourable as the two previous decades for the advance of organizational democracy. A long period of earlier institutional expansion reflected full employment and economic growth which had raised the expectations of the workforce on control questions and on participation in rewards from work. But more latterly, high unemployment has undoubtedly weakened organized labour. And, in such a situation, managements have been increasingly able to reassert a high degree of control over the labour process. Moreover, although by means of the legislature governmental intervention in industrial relations has continued apace, the avowedly anti-corporatist ideologies of the 1980s have reduced the pressure to accommodate organized labour through participation in the decision-making and control structures of the firm.

For 'cyclical' theorists, then, the current era is unfavourable for progress towards organizational democracy. But equally there is no reason to suppose that the future heralds a linear long-term *retreat* from employee participation. Indeed, on the basis of historical precedent, a further upsurge of interest in the years ahead can be anticipated.

The favourable conjunctures approach

But while it is accepted here that the search for a smooth 'onward and upward' trend towards organizational democracy is likely to prove fruitless, a number of broad patterns of advance can be delineated. Indeed, as we shall see, there have been three principal cumulative waves during the current century (the first two associated with control and the third with ownership). Moreover, the bulk of the institutionalized forms of participatory democracy have been durable, even though actual worker influence over decision making has fluctuated appreciably depending upon changes in the power of organized labour.

The 'favourable conjunctures' thesis thus encapsulates the notion of an uneven but advancing pattern which depends greatly on variations in circumstance and situation between and within particular nations. In particular, international differences in practice are recognized and are seen to reflect diverse cultural and ideological conditions; complexities in the relationships of power between the state, employers, and trade unions; and distinctive legislative initiatives (Clegg 1976, Poole 1986a, b). More specifically, too, spatial and temporal variations are to be expected in individual countries. Hence, at a given point in time, there will be parts of the economy which are experiencing particularly rapid rates of growth, and where moves towards organizational democracy are, in turn, most likely to occur.

Furthermore, the favourable conjunctures thesis recognizes that historical situations are not necessarily repeated, and hence *different* types of scheme may become ascendant in each distinctive wave of advance. Above all, a sharp distinction is drawn between the integrative and consultative types of institution envisaged in wartime conditions and the disjunctive (trade union-based) forms which familiarly appear in periods of class tension and labour unrest (Cronin 1979, Poole 1982).

The 'favourable conjunctures' thesis also entails the recognition that specific forms of participation may advance or decline in distinctive periods. In particular, a number of practices (notably producer co-operatives) are seen to emerge *counter-cyclically* in: (1) periods of recession; (2) in firms or enterprises in declining sectors of industry; (3) in depressed or periphery economies or regions; and (4) in Third World countries at fairly low levels of development. Similarly, over time, some types of participation (e.g. board-level representation structures based on the trade union channel) will be in decline, whereas others will be appreciably expanding (e.g. managerially initiated schemes for information sharing, consultation, and profit sharing).

Economic and industrial democracy: are they coterminous?

The argument so far is that debates on the origins of economic and industrial democracy may be synthesized by an inclusive theory of organizational democracy premised on the notion of 'favourable conjunctures'. But it must be stressed that economic and industrial democracy are not invariably coterminous. Indeed, there are clearly circumstances in which employee *financial* participation has advanced, even though the *decision-making* involvement of the workforce has not been institutionalized and vice versa. Moreover, even if the two phenomena are broadly linked, this relationship may not apply across a wide spectrum of organizational democracy practices.

Theoretically, there are a number of further relevant points to be made here. First, we can only expect a very close linkage between *specific* forms of economic and industrial democracy. In a

7

classical producer co-operative, it is thus likely that full worker ownership and self-management will be present, but neither is probable in a large-scale publicly quoted company based on shareholder supremacy. Second, a great deal depends on the *originators* of particular types of arrangement. If managements are the main agents, profit sharing and joint consultation may well advance together but board-level participation is not a likely departure. Third, the specific focus of governmental and state supports may be relevant. For example, in the UK, there is legislative underpinning for profit sharing but not for works councils. By contrast, in Sweden, there are statutory provisions for several types of varieties of economic and industrial democracy. Fourth, there is substantial variation historically in any given form of organizational democracy. Thus, the profit-sharing schemes in nineteenth-century Britain are not the same as Inland Revenue-approved save as you earn (SAYE) schemes of the current era. And, fifth, the clustering of particular types of economic and industrial democracy depends fundamentally on common, supportive, background conditions. Collective bargaining arguably involves both reward sharing and participation in decision making; but it can only advance under circumstances which favour trade union growth. By contrast, management seeking to retain a skilled and educated workforce and to use the capacities of their employees to the full may well seek to expand, say, profit-sharing and quality circles as part of an inclusive policy for employee involvement.

The development of profit sharing in Britain

Turning more specifically at this point to examine profit-sharing and employee-shareholding schemes, it is important to appreciate that these forms of economic democracy have had a long and interesting history. It is reasonable to argue that, so far as the *adoption* of schemes is concerned, 'cyclical' theories have received considerable support from the historical record up until the recent past. However, the circumstances of the 1980s have been very different from the earlier periods of advance and undoubtedly reveal radically different favourable conditions. Moreover, even when the *adoption* of schemes has declined (in situations which are consistent with a 'cyclical' interpretation), it is important to note that many existing arrangements within companies have remained. For much of the twentieth century, then, there has not been any dramatic decline in the actual practice of profit sharing and employee share ownership in British companies but, arguably, an *uneven* pattern of long-term advance.

It is interesting to note that the development of profit sharing in the nineteenth century was criticized by many of the most influential figures in the labour movement. Thus, for Marx (1858: 288), profit sharing was to be regarded 'as a special way of cheating the workers and of *deducting a part of their wages* in the more precarious form of a profit depending on the state of the business'. Moreover, the views of the Webbs were particularly trenchant and incisive; for they viewed profit-sharing and share-ownership schemes as fundamentally opposed to the principles of collective bargaining and trade unionism. This was partly because of the reduction of labour mobility (necessary for the employee to make the best possible bargain with the employer), but more especially on account of the way in which these schemes were likely to destroy the 'community of interests' upon which successful collective bargaining ultimately depends. Moreover, because profit-sharing schemes are typically unilaterally imposed on workers, in their view, there was no reason to suppose that the return on shares or profits would be maintained or that employees would receive a worthwhile allocation from their respective employers (Webb and Webb 1920).

But these objections appear to have had no appreciable effect on the advance of employee financial participation. In the nineteenth century there were thus a number of waves of advance, linked with four main conditions: (1) a 'philanthropic' outlook amongst certain employers; (2) economic buoyancy; (3) the rise of trade unions; and (4) industrial unrest.

The first epoch of development occurred between 1865 and 1873 when at least twenty-five employers in Britain introduced profit sharing and other forms of industrial partnership (see Brannen 1983). The experiment pioneered by Henry Briggs, Son and Co., a colliery firm in Yorkshire, was a particularly important example. Indeed, in 1865 it had been converted into a joint stock company and not only invited employees to take up shares but also, in 1869, called upon the mineworkers who were shareholders to elect one of their number to be a director (Phelps Brown 1960: 210). The scheme at Whitworth was another path-breaking initiative which it was hoped would 'resolve many of the fears associated with the growth of limited liability and remote direction of the company' (Melling 1983: 62).

There can be little doubt that 'philanthropic' managements were partly responsible for the emergence of the early schemes. After all, the eras of advance of profit sharing have closely paralleled the extension of welfare provisions within companies, and it was typically only in firms in which the employer's 'social conscience' had been aroused that experimentation in employee financial participation took place (Melling 1983). Yet favourable economic conditions, increasing trade union activity, and industrial disputes were also connected with the early waves of profit sharing and employee share ownership (see Ramsay 1977). And there is no doubt that worsening trade conditions were basic to the demise of many of the early experiments such as that at Briggs, Son and Co., as Ramsay (1977: 484) has documented:

> the scheme foundered when a renewal of recession conditions in 1874 led to a coal masters' move to cut wages. Like their fellows, Briggs' colliers struck in response. The arbitrator supported the masters' demand for a large wage reduction and at the same time the profit sharing scheme was dropped, at the shareholders' insistence, for failing to resolve industrial conflict.

The next wave of advance of profit sharing in Britain occurred between 1889 and 1892 when no less than eighty-eight schemes were initiated. These later practices were undoubtedly affected by structural changes in management manifested in 'the rise of employers' organisations and the ascendancy of a determined managerial leadership' (Melling 1983: 62). Nowhere was this more evident than in the South Metropolitan Gas Company scheme, which was inaugurated in 1889 and pioneered by the Chairman, George Livesey. He had argued the case for profit sharing in paternalistic terms as a means of forestalling trade union organization (Church 1971, Bristow 1974). Moreover, employee financial participation was reflected in a growing coherence in business welfare policies designed to secure the loyalty of the workforce, to maintain managerial legitimacy and to assert 'workplace control' (Melling 1983). Once again, this second wave (and the periods of advance of profit sharing in 1908–9 and 1912–14) occurred in conditions of relative economic buoyancy, trade union advance, and labour unrest.

Prior to the First World War, then, the development of profit sharing had been affected greatly by changes in the business cycle – a dependency which had resulted in a high rate of failure of early experiments. Church (1971: 15) has thus documented that, in 1912, 163 known schemes had been terminated (the average duration of any given arrangement being 12 years). Nevertheless, there were still at least 133 firms with schemes in existence at this particular era of British history.

Immediately following the First World War, there was a dramatic upsurge in profit-sharing schemes accompanying the post-war boom, the rise of trade unionism, and substantial industrial

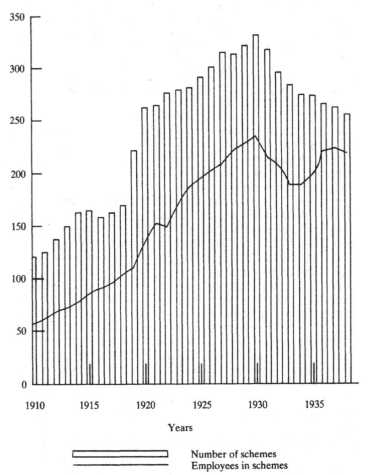

Figure 1.2　Profit-sharing schemes and employees: 1910–38

Number of schemes/employees (000's)

Years

Number of schemes
Employees in schemes

Source: Matthews (1988).

militancy. This is shown in figure 1.2 in which the strong increase in the adoption of schemes in 1919 and 1920 is revealed. Indeed, sixty-two schemes were started in 1919 and fifty-eight in 1920, in firms as diverse as Bryant and May, Westminster and Parr's Bank, and the Distiller's company. Moreover, growth continued up until 1930, not least because of the tendency for developments in a given firm in a particular industry to occasion the adoption of similar schemes in competitor companies. Hence, amongst the chocolate makers, Rowntree was the first to introduce a scheme in 1923, but this initiative was rapidly followed by Cadbury in the same year and Needlers the year after (see Matthews 1988). Moreover, an important scheme developed at Imperial Chemical Industries (ICI) in the late 1920s from one of its constituent companies, Brunner Mond Ltd. Under this arrangement, workers could buy company shares at a special discount (Ramsay and Haworth 1984: 303–4).

Following the onset of depression and a considerable reduction in both trade union density and the incidence of industrial conflict, the 1930s were to witness a considerable fall in the rate of adoption of profit-sharing schemes. However, it is important to note that, despite this decline, there were considerably more schemes in existence throughout the 1930s than, say, in the period of 1910–20 (see figure 1.2). To be sure, no schemes at all were introduced in 1933, but there was a later revival in the 1930s occasioned by the introduction of profit sharing at the Vauxhall motor company in 1935 and in Morris the year later (see Matthews 1988).

Indeed, there were a number of distinctive characteristics of the depression years which, as we shall see, are highly relevant to understanding the current wave of advance of profit sharing and employee share ownership. First of all, while there was a substantial decline in 'staple' industries (such as coal, shipbuilding, textiles, and iron and steel), there was also a series of expanding industries (such as motor vehicles and chemicals) where labour conditions were appreciably different. This uneven pattern of industrial development occasioned substantial regional inequalities of a type familiar today (see Jones and Pool 1940). Second, there was evidence of an appreciable effect of technology on labour relations in industries where mechanization and rationalization were proceeding apace. And, third, it was entirely consistent for there to be difficulties in obtaining certain types of skilled and educated workers in advancing industries and regions, despite the existence of massive unemployment in the declining areas. In short, managerial interest in profit sharing varied appreciably depending upon the diverse economic, technological, and labour market conditions which obtained in this era.

Following the Second World War, there was a further advance in profit sharing and employee shareholding accompanying the more favourable economic circumstances of the period. In a survey carried out in 1954, the Ministry of Labour discovered that about 500 companies practised some form of profit sharing. Moreover, in an early study by Copeman (1958), a rich variety of forms of profit sharing were discovered, including: the straightforward use of profit sharing; the employee investing some savings in the company in return for an extra-high yield on the investment; the creation of an employee share trust which denied the employee full shareholding rights; and access to ordinary stock which the employee could purchase at a price below market value.

Of signal importance in this period was the development of the ICI scheme in 1953 which extended the system of allowing employees to purchase company shares at a discount rate to allow for an annual distribution of shares to workers depending on profit levels (in the next two decades about thirty-six million shares were distributed in this way) (see Ramsay and Haworth 1984: 304). And, in 1958, the Wider Share Ownership Council was established with the objective of stimulating profit sharing and employee shareholding (see Copeman *et al.* 1984).

But the modern spectacular advance of employee financial participation, which will be documented in detail in chapter three, was occasioned largely by the passage of the 1978 Finance Act. This marked a major change in the impetus for the development of schemes since governmental and legislative support for profit sharing and employee shareholding was now forthcoming. To be sure, in 1972, the Conservative Chancellor of the Exchequer, Anthony Barber, had offered tax concessions for share option and incentive schemes (and this was extended in 1973 to enable employees to purchase shares in their companies on a SAYE basis). But, following Liberal pressure in the period of the Lib–Lab pact, it was the Labour Chancellor, Denis Healey, who initiated the legislation which underpins the current wave of profit-sharing and share-ownership schemes. Thus, under the provisions of the 1978 Act, income tax exemptions are available for schemes which receive Inland Revenue approval. These approved profit-sharing (APS) schemes involve companies allocating profits to a trust fund which acquires shares in that firm on behalf of the employees.

The Conservative government which commenced office in 1979 substantially improved these profit-sharing arrangements in 1980,

The origins of economic democracy

1982, and 1983. The 1980 Finance Act in particular made provision
for Inland Revenue-approved SAYE share-option schemes, whereby
the employee is given the option of buying shares at a fixed price
providing that the shares are bought from the proceeds of SAYE
contracts. The terms of the savings contract are normally envisaged to be for five or seven years. At the end of this period,
employees either buy the shares (at the price fixed on commence-
ment of the savings contract) or take their savings and any bonus
in cash. Moreover, the Finance Act of 1984 provided firms with a
further major incentive to develop discretionary, and particularly
Executive Share-option (ESO), schemes that allow senior personnel
in the company to exercise options to buy shares. To take up this
option, the employee pays on exercise the full market value of the
shares at the time that the option was granted.

International developments

But the advance in profit-sharing and employee-shareholding
schemes that has been characteristic of Britain's industrial relations
in the 1980s has also been experienced in a number of other
countries. Hence, even though it is not the purpose of this study to
undertake a comprehensive comparative analysis of employee
financial participation, it is essential to say something at this point,
if only rather briefly, about the world-wide nature of the movement. The analysis commences with a brief assessment of the
experience of twenty-three different industrial and developing
countries. This is followed by a more detailed examination of the
diverse experiences in the United States, West Germany, and
Sweden.

The widespread advance of profit-sharing and employee share-
ownership schemes in the 1980s may be interpreted as part of three
distinctive waves of development of organizational democracy
dur ng the twentieth century. The first two movements were
associated with managerial control in the firm and were designed
to accelerate the growth of industrial democracy, while the third
has been linked with ownership and with the spread of economic
democracy. Indeed, as Abell (1985: 53–4) has noted, these primary
international waves may be characterized as follows:

Wave 1. 1915–55: the rise of statutory or voluntary works
councils and similar machinery at plant level in both market
and planned economies.

Wave 2. 1920 onwards but particularly since 1945: the
emergence of board-level co-determination culminating in the

14

EEC Fifth directive which is aimed to make such arrangements mandatory in all European member states.

Wave 3. 1980s: the extension of ownership rights to both management and labour. The growth of stock-option schemes, management and labour buyouts, capital ownership and wage-earner funds, and producer co-operatives.

Nevertheless, if we examine the international experience of employee financial participation, it is clear that development has been uneven and, in many countries, it still remains an uncommon feature of the industrial relations landscape. Table 1.1 thus sets out the situation with respect to profit sharing, employee participation, and the broader industrial relations background of a wide range of nations. It will be noted that in Australia, Denmark, France, Japan, New Zealand, Norway, Portugal, Spain, the UK, and the USA, schemes are either already well established or there has been substantial interest in recent years. However, in the West European countries of Ireland, Italy, Luxembourg, the Netherlands, Switzerland, and West Germany, there has not been an appreciable expansion of profit sharing and share ownership in the 1980s. Moreover, in most of the industrializing, developing countries (e.g. Hong Kong, Malaysia, Singapore, and Thailand) schemes remain uncommon except, in some cases, for those designed for senior executives.

The uneven pattern of advance of profit sharing and share ownership is reinforced by the substantial diversity of worker participation practices and of industrial relations more generally. It is arguable that, in countries with a particularly rapid expansion of employee financial participation, the arrangements for industrial democracy are either highly advanced or in a process of expansion. But, as we shall see from the West German case, until recently this situation certainly did not universally obtain. Moreover, although profit sharing has clearly grown most rapidly in the mature industrial societies, it is undoubtedly compatible with a wide variety of industrial relations systems (centralized or decentralized, legally regulated or voluntaristic, high or low levels of union density, and diverse patterns of strike activity).

The United States

To highlight the varied world-wide patterns of employee financial participation, three detailed cases are examined at this point. Beginning with the USA, there is no doubt that there have been appreciable changes both in profit sharing and employee

Table 1.1 The international experience of employee financial participation

Country	Profit-sharing arrangements	Employee participation arrangements	Industrial relations background
Australia	Encouraged by government; schemes are growing especially if linked with long-term incentives	Encouraged by both government and unions; a wide range of developments	Hancock report in 1985 supported existing conciliation and arbitration system
Belgium	Schemes still uncommon	Not actively encouraged by government; union involvement in social welfare issues	Union representation required by law for companies with over 50 employees
Denmark	Active support by government encouraging unions to discuss this issue. Some companies have launched their own schemes	Active encouragement by government and unions. Employees have legal right to elect two members of the Board in companies with 50 or more employees	Moves to collective bargaining following governmental attempts to dictate maximum salary increases
Finland	Schemes uncommon but developing	Active encouragement by government and unions. Union consultation an integral part of a company's decision making by law	Agreements traditionally highly centralized
France	Schemes common and encouraged by government	Worker participation encouraged by government and unions and is covered by legislation	Depending on size of company, unions have a legal right to put up their own candidates to staff representation committees
Germany (Federal Republic)	Profit sharing still not common but developing	Worker participation (works councils and codetermination) legal and mandatory in all but the smaller firms	A company with more than 500 employees has to have a union committee
Hong Kong	Profit sharing uncommon	Unions actually limited but worker participation encouraged	Co-operative employer–employee relations
Ireland (Republic of)	Schemes exist in a few companies but bonuses more common	Worker participation actively encouraged by government and unions. Most state enterprises	Focus on job preservation; system of labour courts under scrutiny

Country			
		have union representation at board level	
Italy	Schemes uncommon but management share-option schemes have recently expanded	Encouraged by unions	Large union federations linked with political divisions in the country
Japan	Increasing emphasis in companies to encourage employees to purchase shares	Accepted as inherent to every aspect of business life	Company-based unions
Luxembourg	Schemes uncommon	Active encouragement by government and unions. Works councils required by law in all companies with more than 150 employees	Union representation required by law in companies with more than 15 employees
Malaysia	Schemes uncommon	Encouraged by unions but not by government	Emphasis on stability and co-operation in industrial relations
The Netherlands	Schemes uncommon	Active encouragement by government and unions. Elected works councils	Considerable union–employer co-operation
New Zealand	Not common but expanding	Increased concern for industrial democracy in recent years	Union representation in companies now compulsory in larger and medium-size firms
Norway	Profit sharing increasingly popular	Active encouragement by government and unions	Employee representation on company boards required by law where there are 50 or more employees
Portugal	Profit sharing not common but increasingly being considered	Legislation regulating participation levels still to be implemented	Official controls on level of union representation in the company
Singapore	Profit sharing not common	Government encouragement of harmonious industrial relations; unions keen to be active in companies	Largely strike-free country. Industrial Dialogue Committees formed

Country	Profit-sharing arrangements	Employee participation arrangements	Industrial relations background
Spain	Profit sharing common and actively encouraged by the government	Worker participation encouraged by both government and unions	Trade unions linked with political parties
Sweden	Active and increasing interest in profit-sharing and share-ownership schemes	Several laws on worker participation; all companies employing more than 50 employees are required to have union representation on the Board	Centralized industrial relations; the idea of collective labour funds led to conflict
Switzerland	Profit sharing uncommon	Worker participation encouraged by unions but not by government	Emphasis on co-operation in union–management relations
Thailand	Profit sharing uncommon but does exist for senior executives	Unions not actively encouraged	Unemployment weakens labour; unions only really powerful in state enterprises
United Kingdom	Profit-sharing and employee share-ownership schemes expanded appreciably in the 1980s	Increase in job-related participation schemes but less enthusiasm for board-level participation by comparison with the 1970s	Disputes declining overall, but large stoppages occurred in the 1980s. Union membership declining
United States of America	Profit-sharing and share-ownership schemes very common	Employee participation has spread at a rapid rate in the USA in the 1970s and 1980s	Low level of strikes but those which do occur are of long duration – union locals more important than national federations

Source: Based on *Industrial Participation* (1985–6: 17–25).

involvement in recent years. These developments have accompanied a rapid change in the industrial relations system which had remained stable for approximately the thirty previous years.

It was one of the founding economic principles of the USA that the ownership of capital should be broadly dispersed. Indeed it was believed that 'broad ownership of capital would lead to a more productive economy, a more equitable society, and an involved stable citizenry' (Klein and Rosen 1986: 387). But while these formative ideologies of American society have remained favourable to worker participation in ownership for more than three centuries, until relatively recently few employees had an equity stake in their companies. Indeed, in the early 1970s, 1 per cent of the population owned 50 per cent of privately owned wealth.

This is not of course to suggest that employee financial participation is a novel departure in the USA. Indeed, it is possible to isolate several historical developments. These are set out in table 1.2 where it will be noted that, in the nineteenth century, there were a number of short-lived craft co-operatives established in New England in the 1850s; together with the birth of organizational co-operatives in the mid-western farmlands in the late 1860s and early 1870s. Various profit-sharing schemes emerged in the late nineteenth and early twentieth centuries, followed by the formation of plywood co-ops in the north-west around 1930. Since the Second World War, pension-fund plans in industry emerged and later, in the 1960s, the so-called 'counter-culture' co-ops were a further notable development.

The current upsurge of interest in employee financial participation in the USA has been fuelled by two principal changes: (1) the emergence of 'buyouts' or industrial worker ownership in response to plant shutdowns; and (2) the legislation that has encouraged the formation of Employee Stock-ownership Plans (ESOPs).

Worker 'buyouts' of plants began to be quite common in the USA in the 1970s, accompanying the demise of the so-called 'smoke stack industries'. Rosen *et al.* (1986) have revealed that at least sixty-five 'buyouts' took place between 1971 and 1975, most of which occurred in firms in traditional activities which were experiencing acute financial difficulties. To begin with, 'buyouts' met with considerable success, although early optimism has been frequently succeeded by disillusionment and with surprisingly little change in control patterns within the firm.

A particularly well documented case is the Rath Meat Packing Company which was transferred to worker ownership in 1979. Against a background of an appreciable decline in the fortunes of

19

Table 1.2 Key phases in the development of employee participation in ownership in the USA

1850	1870	1900	1930	1950	1960	1970	1975
Short-lived rise of craft co-ops in New England		Evolution of various profit-sharing schemes	Formation of plywood co-ops in north-west		Rise of counter-culture collectives, producer, and consumer co-ops		ESOP legislation passed into law
	Birth of agricultural co-ops in mid-western farmlands			Development of pension-fund plans in industry		Emergence of industrial worker ownership in response to plant shutdowns	

Source: Woodworth (1981: 50).

the meat packing industry, the union agreed to accept substantial wage and fringe benefit cuts in return for 60 per cent of the stock in the firm. However, despite a series of changes (including at one point the union president assuming the company presidency), in January 1985 the plant ceased trading altogether (see Hammer 1985, Hammer and Strauss 1986).

Worker 'buyouts' of existing plants have thus met with mixed success in the USA. But the rise of ESOP companies has been spectacular and without any severe checks on growth and expansion. An ESOP enables employees to acquire a substantial stake in the equity of the employing company. In detail, as the Income Data Services Report (1987: 29) has indicated:

> A company or its employees establishes a trust (similar to that used to hold shares under the Inland Revenue approved deferred profit-sharing trusts) which holds the equity on behalf of employees.
>
> The trust uses money, normally provided by an external lending institution such as a bank, to buy shares in the company on behalf of employees. These shares may be purchased from other shareholders, either directly or through the market, or they may be newly-issued. Dividends on the shares, together with any capital gains realised, can be used to redeem borrowings. The borrowing can be further reduced by companies paying a proportion of their profits into the trust, or employees contributing through a share option or profit sharing scheme.

The impetus for the growth of ESOPs came from the attorney, Louis Kelso, who, with the enthusiastic support of Senator Russell Long, was able to propose a series of laws that gave a substantial stimulus to employee financial participation. By the mid 1980s, the spread of ESOPs had been so remarkable that it was estimated that over 8 million workers in 8,000 companies were covered by employee share-ownership schemes. Moreover, ESOP firms have almost certainly grown more rapidly than their competitors and are generally viewed as having higher rates of profitability and more adaptable workforces (though the evidence here is not entirely consistent; see Whyte *et al.* 1983, Tannenbaum *et al.* 1984, Rosen *et al.* 1986, Hammer and Strauss 1986).

Moreover, it is clear that, despite a number of precedents, the recent history of the USA reveals a period of more rapid growth of interest in employee financial participation than in any previous era. And the American case reinforces the view that developments in Britain are part of a much broader change in advanced industrial societies towards profit sharing and employee share ownership in the firm.

West Germany

But West Germany has been, until recently, a major exception. The high level of industrial relations consensus linked with the need to rebuild a war-shattered economy has generally been identified as conducive to the institutionalization of worker participation in decision making and reflected in comprehensive legislation covering works councils and co-determination (IDE 1981a). However, the moves to equity participation by employees in the Federal Republic of Germany have been far more circumscribed.

The available evidence from West Germany suggests that employee stock-ownership schemes were once a rare phenomenon. In a study carried out in the 1970s, Guski and Schneider (1977) discovered only fourteen firms in which employees held more than 50 per cent of the equity. Unlike North America, these types of companies did not appear with greater frequency in the recession (indeed there was a modest decline after 1972). Moreover, most schemes had arisen from companies making provisions for equity participation through profit sharing rather than from employee-initiated 'buyouts'.

These findings were largely corroborated by a later study by Gurdon (1985). Indeed, he discovered no evidence of an appreciable expansion of schemes in the 1980s, and the cases which had occurred largely reflected a 'revolution from the top' in which 'the initiative for change came from the original owner' (Gurdon 1985: 120).

Moreover, there are strong grounds for concluding that the extensive network of support for protecting employment and for the institutionalization of workplace industrial relations once operated against the development of 'grass-roots' forms of equity participation in West Germany. Plant-closure decisions are more easily reversed in Germany than in Britain or the USA and there is a strong disincentive to worker 'buyouts' because, under bankruptcy laws, the new owner of a firm must assume all liabilities personally. Further obstacles to equity participation include

> the lack of government support either in the form of fiscal encouragement to workers and employees to broaden investment in enterprise equity or through a coherent programme of loan guarantees for buyouts; the complexity of German company law; and the antipathy of influential unions. (Gurdon 1985: 126)

Hence, while interest in profit-sharing and employee share-ownership schemes has been recently growing, in contrast with the extensive industrial democracy provisions, there had been little acceleration in the advance of equity participation by employees up until the mid 1980s in West Germany.

Sweden

In Sweden, there is comprehensive legislation on worker partici-pation in decision making coupled with widespread interest in economic democracy. Against the backcloth of an historical com-promise between the contending parties to industrial relations and the Basic Agreement of 1938, a series of enactments covering worker participation in decision making have been concluded in Sweden. The post-war legislation began with the Works Council Agreement 1946 and, in the 1970s, there was a thorough transfor-mation of labour legislation culminating in the passage of the Co-determination Act in 1977. This made provision for the establishment of works councils, information sharing on economic questions, the right of employees in firms with more than twenty-five employees to elect two delegates to the Board, and an extension of the collective bargaining rights of local unions (IDE 1981a: 58):

> The 1976 report demanded that every privately owned firm should use 20 per cent of its profits to issue shares, which should be owned by the wage earners collectively through one central fund for the whole country. The central fund should be headed by a board appointed by the national unions. The right to nominate members of company boards should be reserved to the local unions as long as the wage earners' fund owned no more than 20 per cent of the shares. After that the right should be switched to a number of branch funds, appointed by the national unions.

Proposals for such a radical transformation in the ownership and control of capital in Swedish industry and society were met with unbridled opposition from the employers' associations and rather different ideas were subsequently formulated. Following a series of changes (and the electoral defeat of the Social Democratic Party in 1976), employee participation in capital formation through 'wage-earner' funds was not finally enacted until 1983. On the basis of this Act, funds are derived from two sources (a payroll tax of 1 per cent and a one-fifth levy on employers which make 'excess' profits of over 15–20 per cent). Moreover, the Regional Councils

23

which are responsible for the funds 'divide the powers accruing to shares with the employees in the company where the shares have been purchased' (Ramsay and Haworth 1984: 311), a measure which has reduced the role of trade unions in the administration of funds. However, notwithstanding these modifications to the original Meidner proposals, the notion of employee participation in capital formation through 'wage-earner' funds is far more radical in conception than the current provisions for profit sharing and employee share ownership in Britain and the USA. Different political configurations and the strength of the Swedish labour movement underlie these diverse experiences. But the Swedish case provides a vivid contrast to West Germany since it reveals that the institutionalization of industrial democracy can be readily accompanied by legislative provisions for involving employees in ownership and capital formation in industry and society.

Conclusion

Following a conceptual classification, the objective of the introductory chapter has been to illustrate the long history and the rich variety of international practices in employee financial participation. Despite the oscillating movements over time, the 1980s have undoubtedly been a period of spectacular advance in profit-sharing and share-ownership schemes; a situation occasioned above all by positive support from governments and the legislature. At this juncture, it is appropriate to establish a series of theoretical propositions to account for the principal variations which obtain between particular nations and amongst different industries and services in any one country.

Chapter two

Explanatory frameworks

Under what conditions are schemes for profit sharing and employee share ownership likely to emerge? What circumstances propel the managements of particular firms to adopt schemes while their counterparts in the same industrial sector decide against such a course of action? These central questions are now addressed. A number of explanatory frameworks are established which are subjected to a more rigorous empirical analysis in the subsequent chapters of the monograph.

Amongst the many attempts to grapple with these important questions, two broad approaches may be identified. The first is a politico-economic theory of diversity and is essentially 'structuralist' in compass. More specifically, it infers that outcomes are the product of governmental action and economic 'infrastructure'. And these forces are seen to be ones over which members of organizations have very little influence, if any at all. In short, these conditions are viewed as largely determining the development of employee financial participation irrespective of human choice.

The second approach is based on *action* premises and focuses, in the first instance, on the *choices* of key personnel in the enterprise. It recognizes the importance of governmental initiatives and economic 'infrastructural' factors. Nevertheless, these are viewed as either *facilitating* or *constraining* choices but not determining them. Managers are accredited a central role in the genesis of schemes (hence their strategies and 'styles' are of vital consequence). But their choices are in turn seen to be affected by: (1) their own ideologies and values on these issues; (2) other elements in the 'climate' of industrial relations (such as the preference for developing organizational democracy in general and for variable payment systems); and (3) the power and strategies of other organized groups (this applies particularly to trade unions, staff associations, and employees themselves). Moreover, trade union and employee views are in turn seen to be influenced by broader

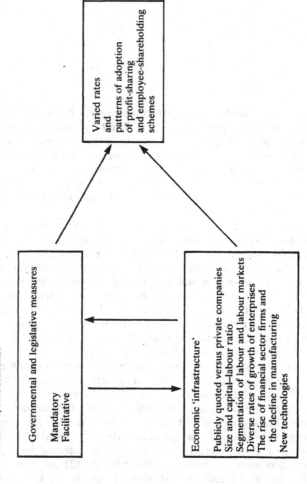

Figure 2.1 A framework for analysing employee financial participation: model A, structuralist

Varied rates and patterns of adoption of profit-sharing and employee-shareholding schemes

Governmental and legislative measures

Mandatory
Facilitative

Economic 'infrastructure'

Publicly quoted versus private companies
Size and capital–labour ratio
Segmentation of labour and labour markets
Diverse rates of growth of enterprises
The rise of financial sector firms and
   the decline in manufacturing
New technologies

Figure 2.2 A framework for analysing employee financial participation: model B, action

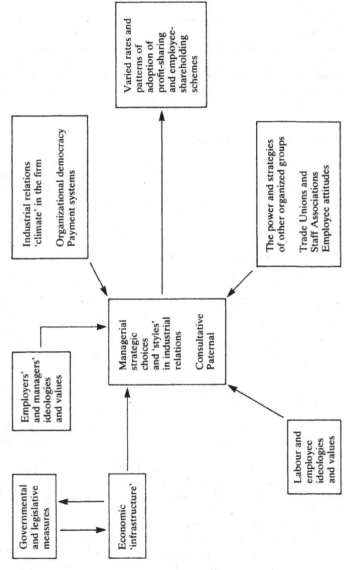

ideologies and values which affect these particular groups and individuals.

As will become clear from the empirical sections, in our view, the second approach receives by far the greatest support, even though a one-sidedly 'subjectivist' argument taking no account of the constraints on choice would certainly not be sustained from the available data. The two main approaches are set out in the frameworks in figures 2.1 and 2.2, the main elements of each position being enumerated in the account which follows.

Government and the legislature

It has been one of the main findings of cross-national empirical research that organizational democracy is enhanced by what have been termed 'external support systems'. Moreover, these have been found to stem primarily from either: (1) favourable legislation based on governmental initiatives; or (2) the organized power of wider labour movements (IDE 1979, 1981a). More specifically, there can be little doubt that the rise of employee financial participation in the 1980s has been facilitated by favourable legislation. The importance of the various Finance Acts in Britain has already been stressed and, indeed, the wave of development of profit sharing and share ownership in many countries can be traced in part to facilitative governmental measures.

The explanation for profit sharing and employee share ownership in terms of governmental supports is likely to apply to two main types of variation: (1) the differences amongst countries; (2) the changing patterns in a single country over a period of time. The first case is most obviously evident in the contrast between countries where such arrangements are mandatory (e.g. Sweden) and those with only voluntary provisions (e.g. UK, USA). And the second is illustrated by countries such as the UK where the modern rise of profit sharing is distinctive in a number of respects from the earlier waves of advance in the nineteenth and twentieth centuries. This is apparent in the current obligation upon companies to obtain Inland Revenue approval for any tax-exempt schemes.

Yet as an explanation for variations within a single country at a given point in time, the thesis based on governmental and legislative intervention is less satisfactory. It may be in part valid in accounting for differences between publicly quoted companies and private concerns. Moreover, it is arguable that legislative provisions for profit sharing typically favour firms with high capital–labour ratios. But outside these two limiting cases, it is necessary for a 'structuralist' analysis to identify specific economic and technological factors to develop a better understanding of the origins of spatial differences in the adoption of profit-sharing and employee-shareholding schemes.

Economic 'infrastructure'

The underlying material forces in any given society are of course dynamic and constantly changing. At any specific point in time, some parts of an economy will be experiencing rapid advance while others are in terminal decline. The situation of large publicly quoted companies will be different from that of the small private concern. Labour markets may be becoming increasingly segmented. And structural shifts (from, say, manufacturing to private financial services) may be part of a transformative process towards post-industrial societies.

As a consequence, the situation of any given company may well be markedly different from that experienced by another concern in the same economic system. This applies not only to the highly contrasting circumstances of, say, the traditional manufacturing firm and the service enterprise, but also to undertakings with different degrees of technological sophistication in the same industrial sector and to companies of diverse sizes and ownership patterns.

Such differences are almost certainly germane to understanding variations in the development of profit-sharing and employee share-ownership schemes in a single country. But to assess the so-called 'economic infrastructure' thesis in more detail the argument is presented under six main heads: (1) the distinction between publicly quoted and private companies; (2) the size effect and the importance of capital–labour ratio; (3) the segmentation of labour and labour markets; (4) diverse rates of growth in different sectors of the economy; (5) the decline of manufacturing and rise of services and especially those in the finance sector; and (6) the impact of new technologies and their related 'human-resource' requirements.

Publicly quoted versus private companies

At any given point in time, there are different types of ownership that coexist in given economic systems. These include the nationalized corporations, publicly quoted companies technically owned by shareholders, private firms, management-owned firms (following buyouts), and employee-owned enterprises (such as worker buyouts and producer co-operatives). Moreover, there are strong grounds for supposing that these diverse modes of ownership are interlinked with profit sharing and share ownership for employees.

The 'economic infrastructure' thesis thus involves the assumption that the ownership of a given company is vital to the advance or otherwise of employee financial participation. The nationalized or publicly owned concern is not seen as readily amenable to profit sharing or employee share ownership unless it is converted to a producer co-operative. By contrast, both management- or worker-owned (buyout) enterprises and producer co-operatives are, by definition, highly conducive to employee financial participation (though, in most countries, the percentage of firms under such arrangements remains small). Finally, publicly quoted companies are viewed as more likely to adopt share-based profit sharing than their privately owned counterparts. This stems partly from legislation for employee shareholding being particularly tailored to the large publicly quoted company, partly from managerial professionalism (knowledge of schemes and how to develop them is particularly likely in such concerns), and partly because the small-scale proprietor may not wish to issue shares at all, let alone to develop complex schemes for profit sharing. On the other hand, *cash-based* profit sharing is not in principle impeded by the firm being privately owned.

Size and capital–labour ratio

The different modes of ownership are also interlinked with varying patterns of enterprise size and ratios of capital to labour. Indeed, a further proposition of the 'economic infrastructure' thesis is that the larger the size of the company and the higher its capital–labour ratio, the more likely it is that employee financial participation will become an established practice.

The effects of scale of industrial operations have been observed over a wide range of industrial relations phenomenon (see, for example, Brown 1981). Moreover, so far as employee financial participation is concerned, larger-scale enterprises are more likely than smaller firms to have schemes because: (1) professionalized managers in specialist financial and personnel departments will be able to frame complex arrangements, understand the minutiae of the legislation, and be fully appraised of the tax advantages of schemes; (2) company-based wage and salary systems will be common and these may lead to profit-sharing arrangements; (3)

labour will be more organized and trade unions or staff associations may press for such measures; and (4) managements will fashion industrial relations strategies, in which employee financial participation may be a signal feature. Nevertheless, in some cases, capital–labour ratio rather than size *per se* may be particularly relevant to the genesis of schemes because employees in firms with a large capital base are able to build up appreciable shareholdings without any consequential dilution of the rights of existing shareholders (which in the UK are, of course, protected by means of Investment Protection Committee guidelines).

The segmentation of labour and labour markets

The economic 'infrastructure' thesis requires that account must also be taken of the increasingly complex character of labour and labour markets in advanced industrial societies. More specifically, it infers that schemes for employee financial participation are most likely to advance in companies where: (1) labour is highly skilled and educated and relatively scarce; and (2) there is an appreciable and readily identifiable core labour force in the enterprise concerned.

For over two decades, then, it has been appreciated that segmentation has occasioned at least two qualitatively distinct, non-convergent labour markets: primary and secondary (Doeringer and Piore 1971). The first comprises jobs with high pay, good promotional prospects and seniority, and typically strong labour organizations. The second encompasses the poor jobs sector with low pay, limited opportunities for promotion, the continuing threat of redundancy, ineffective unions, and a high proportion of female and immigrant labour. Moreover, the characteristics of each market are seen to lead to fundamentally different work experiences for 'primary' and 'secondary' workers respectively (Gordon *et al.* 1982). More latterly, this mode of analysis has been applied to the identification of more complex labour segments (notably independent and subordinate primary occupations, linked with diverse skills and the new technologies), and with the substantial expansion of part-time working (Rubery *et al.* 1984).

The upshot of these developments has been a highly diverse experience of those in employment and in the relationship of companies to the labour market. More specifically, even in a period of major recession and unemployment, there have been areas (such as in the financial services) where there have been actual labour shortages and where managements might be expected to seek to retain a labour force by means of profit sharing and other similar incentives. This has contrasted with firms in which the core of primary workers has been diminishing, where labour shedding has been on a substantial scale, and where the new jobs that have emerged have been in secondary, part-time employment.

Diverse rates of economic growth

Economic complexity also applies to diverse patterns and rates of growth between different industrial sectors and amongst firms within the same sector. Moreover, on the basis of the economic 'infrastructure' thesis, in expanding firms with high levels of profitability, managements will be the most favourably disposed to advancing schemes for employee financial participation.

Manufacturing, services, and the financial sector

More generally, too, all industrial societies are being gradually replaced by post-industrial structures and institutions. Specifically, there is a decline in the secondary (goods-producing and manu-facturing) sector and its replacement by the tertiary (services such as transportation and utilities), the quaternary (trade, finance, insurance, property), and the quinary sectors (health, education, research, government, recreation, and leisure) (Bell 1973, Kumar 1978). The post-industrial society is not primarily a goods-producing but a service economy with: (1) white-collar workers replacing manual workers as the single largest category in the labour force; (2) the growing predominance of professional, scientific, and technical groups; and (3) the replacement of older, mature technology by information technology (Kumar 1978: 197–8). Moreover, in some countries, such as the UK, exchange rate policies have occasioned substantial deindustrialization, which have had the effect of accelerating a long-term secular movement.

These underlying conditions are potentially germane to the explanation of the uneven advance of profit-sharing and employee-shareholding schemes. The situation in advancing sectors is markedly different from those which are experiencing a substantial decline. Labour market pressures thus act as an incentive to companies to attract and retain an adaptable and educated workforce through share-based schemes. Moreover, novel payment and other reward systems can be introduced far more readily in such situations by comparison with sectors and firms with deeply entrenched collective-bargaining machinery. And this applies especially to the financial sector services in which there is appreciable knowledge of different patterns of incentive and reward.

Similar arguments in principle apply for the comparison of firms in the same sector but with diverse rates of profitability. After all, in highly profitable companies, managements will have an incentive to retain a valued workforce. And they will also be in a position to engage in meaningful profit sharing, while endeavouring to avoid the disincentive effect of making substantial profits but not sharing these with the workforce.

New technology

The economic 'infrastructure' thesis also accommodates the impact of the new technologies on the diverse patterns of adoption of schemes for employee financial participation. However, the arguments here are complex and embrace a number of different dimensions which apply respectively to: (1) firms that are undergoing rapid technological change; and (2) the new technology enterprises themselves.

The introduction of advanced technologies in a given company frequently occasions an increasing polarization between independent and subordinate primary activities. That is to say, whereas some jobs become increasingly skilled and permit a substantial measure of employee autonomy and control, others become deskilled with the task-based participation of the worker being appreciably reduced. The implications for employee financial participation of these changes are probably indirect. But managements may be expected to seek to develop arrangements to cover those in independent primary occupations in order to inculcate a broader commitment to the company, to avoid potentially damaging conflicts, and to prevent the loss of valued employees to competitors.

However, in the new technology firms the adoption of profit-sharing and share-ownership schemes is likely to be integral to company policy. After all, in these enterprises advanced 'human-resourcing' strategies are likely in order to ensure the recruitment and retention of highly skilled and educated personnel required to fill the many primary activities which are being created. Indeed, there is evidence to suggest that, in Silicon Valley-type companies, personnel specialists will foster a wide range of employee-participation practices that encompass 'quality of work-life' programmes and profit sharing (Poole 1984).

Managerial strategic choices and 'styles' in industrial relations

Notwithstanding the central importance of governmental legislation and economic conditions for the rise of employee financial participation, there are nevertheless strong grounds for supposing that these are best viewed as facilitative rather than as actual determinants of outcomes. Indeed, turning to the more specific elements which are unique to an 'action' rather than to a 'structuralist' model, a considerable measure of *choice* in the development of specific arrangements is seen as basic to the overall explanation. Of course, in practice, choices are influenced by distinctive strategies and 'styles' amongst the key personnel involved in industry that may, in turn, reflect broader ideologies and values on labour issues. Given that managements are typically responsible for initiating schemes, the considerations which will bear upon managerial decision making on profit sharing and share ownership are examined at this point.

The background to the formation of distinctive strategies and 'styles' in industrial relations and their impact upon choices with respect to employee financial participation may be understood in terms of the broader ideologies and values of managers themselves. These have arisen in the context of changes in the structure of ownership and in the so-called divorce of ownership from control functions to the modern enterprise. The underlying ideology of managerialism rests on the central tenet that industry should be controlled by those most fitted in terms of natural and acquired abilities; capacities which are, in turn, demonstrated by the professional and technical competence of the individuals concerned. Such deeply rooted values are inconsistent with radical transformation in the structures of control in the modern corporation. But they are conducive to various employee-involvement initiatives such as task-based employee participation, joint consultation, and information sharing. Above all, they are consistent with experimentation with a variety of different incentive and reward systems and, in particular, to the advance of profit-sharing and share-ownership schemes.

Industrial relations strategies refer to long-term policies which are developed by the management of an organization in order to preserve or change the procedures, practices, or results of industrial relations activities over time (Thurley and Wood 1983). They are frequently related to a characteristic decision-making 'style', which refers to the overall approach of companies to labour issues (Poole *et al.* 1982, Purcell and Sisson 1983). In the classic study by Kerr *et al.* (1960), four main 'styles' were identified: authoritarian or directive, paternal, constitutional, and consultative/participative.

And although subsequent research suggests there may be more complex 'hybrid' patterns (Purcell and Sisson 1983), in principle, consultative/participative and paternal 'styles' are likely to be conducive to the extension of profit sharing and share ownership. The reasons for this are complex, but in firms in which consultation and participation in general are encouraged, profit-sharing and shareholding schemes should flourish as extensions of overall policies for stimulating employee involvement. Moreover, in paternal-type companies, financial participation could be expected to be viewed by management as a means of encouraging employee loyalty and the development of the firm's human resources. These objectives may be achieved by discouraging interfirm mobility and by having a commitment to the workforce that extends beyond contractual obligations in actual working time.

Indeed, the view that employee financial participation is furthered by the emergence of distinctive managerial approaches to labour is reinforced by the findings of research. These suggest that both consultative and sophisticated paternal 'styles' of industrial relations management have emerged in many companies in Britain in the 1980s (Brown and Sisson 1984). The first is consistent with the acceptance of collective bargaining but entails attempts by management to focus on individual employees *in addition* to trade union modes of employee involvement. The second reflects the development of advanced personnel techniques designed to preempt collective bargaining and to create long-term employee commitment to the company through security of employment and participation in ownership (Purcell and Sisson 1983, Brown and Sisson 1984).

Industrial relations 'climate' in the firm

A further position is to relate the growth of employee financial participation to broader changes in the industrial relations 'climate' within the firm. Indeed, characteristic sets of attitudes and behaviour are seen as emerging in given companies that encompass distinctive institutional practices over a wide range of management–employee relationships. And, indeed, there has undoubtedly been pressure upon managers in the modern corporation to adopt a far more participatory organizational climate than that obtaining in earlier eras. As Kilmann (1986: 1–2) has observed:

> Creating and then maintaining organizational success is a
> different kind of problem from that of only a few decades ago.
> The world has grown increasingly complex – resulting from
> greater interdependence among world economies. At the same

time, the world has become increasingly dynamic – resulting from the information explosion and worldwide communications. This 'dynamic complexity' means that organisations cannot remain stable for very long. Rather, constant change on the outside requires constant change on the inside. Success is largely determined by how well the organisation adjusts all its tangible and intangible properties to keep itself on track within its surroundings.

The creation of an adaptive modern organization depends of course on a variety of changes in attitudes and institutions. But it is recognized that the advancement of employee involvement in decisions and rewards is central to the 'climate' of the successful company. A participative approach is thus currently recognized as markedly superior to mechanistic authoritarian organizations and is based on the premise that (Kilmann 1986: 20):

> Members throughout the organisations are involved in decision making and implementation on matters that directly concern them. Their insights, expertise, and information are brought to bear on important, complex problems. The executives at the top realise that they have a limited view of the whole situation and purposely search for alternative perspectives. Member involvement in decision making also generates the commitment necessary for successful implementation.

The upshot has been that a wide range of companies have sought to develop an industrial 'climate' in which employee participation has become a signal feature. And this applies not only to decision-making involvement but also to financial participation as well. Indeed, profit-sharing and share-ownership schemes are seen as interlinked with advanced 'human-resourcing' strategies that encourage high levels of performance of people in organizations by reducing conflict, by increasing motivation and satisfaction amongst the workforce, by providing an incentive to work in an adaptable and intelligent fashion, and by enhancing commitment and loyalty to the organization. In short, employee financial participation may be viewed as the product of general company policies on involvement that have resulted in a distinctive industrial relations climate in the advanced and adaptable organizations of the modern era.

Power and strategies of other organized groups

But the capacity of management to develop profit-sharing and share-ownership schemes for employees is also influenced by the power and strategies of other organized groups. This applies particularly of course to the trade unions. Hence a further explanation for the advance of employee financial participation encompasses the role of the other 'actors' in the company's industrial relations system.

At one time, there was a tradition of trade union hostility to profit sharing and employee share ownership. In part the objections raised rested on the preference for collective bargaining which variable patterns of reward were seen to undermine. Schemes for profit sharing were seen to foster an 'illusion of ownership' without providing any real basis for control by workers over their terms and conditions of employment. Moreover, the use of profit sharing by managers in the nineteenth and early twentieth centuries to discourage trade unionism at one time brought schemes into discredit.

Nevertheless, trade union views on profit sharing do not appear to have been antagonistic in the 1980s. Indeed, in the USA, employee stock-ownership plans have been accepted as part of concession bargaining in depressed firms and regions, with profit sharing being viewed as a legitimate union objective, provided it is in addition to adequate wages and fringe benefits (Hammer and Strauss 1986: 21).

The upshot is that the relationship between trade unionism and employee financial participation is likely to be complex. In one view, the presence of trade unions or staff associations may encourage managers to adopt particular types of scheme (Poole 1986b, Stern and McCarthy 1986). After all, managers who recognize and bargain in 'good faith' with trade unions are to be expected to be favourable to participation in general and hence to profit sharing or employee share ownership. But some trade unionists may still be opposed to financial participation schemes, viewing them as enhancing loyalty to the company rather than to the union (hence they may press instead for the extension of collective bargaining and 'constitutional' decision making in the firm). Moreover, the effects of other collectivities (such as staff associations) and of the employees themselves on the development of schemes adds to the complexity, even though favourable attitudes amongst both these groups are likely. And, at all events, a comprehensive explanation for the rise of employee financial participation must in principle take account of the strategies and power of non-managerial groups in the enterprise.

Chapter three

The role of government

In the foregoing chapters, the main argument that has been developed is that the conditions which promote profit sharing and employee shareholding (and, indeed, schemes for organizational democracy more generally) may be best interpreted through the notion of favourable 'conjunctures'. Moreover, whilst there may be a broad evolutionary trend towards the extension of employee involvement in the firm, there are undoubtedly pronounced discontinuities in patterns over time. Furthermore, the favourable 'conjunctures' thesis also points to the probability of substantial variation in the actual adoption of practices in diverse organizations in any given country, as well as considerable international differences in institutional pattern and form at any particular moment in time.

It has also been observed that, so far as the different rates of adoption of profit-sharing and employee-shareholding schemes are concerned, the argument from favourable 'conjunctures' may be elaborated in terms of two basic approaches. The politico-economic or 'structuralist' theory involves the supposition that governmental legislation and economic infrastructural conditions are basic to institutional variation. Furthermore, these forces are viewed as determining outcomes largely independently of the choices of key decision makers in the enterprise itself. By contrast, the 'action' approach entails an initial focus on *strategic choices* at *enterprise level*. These are seen as inevitably producing variations in actual practices. However, such a perspective is not necessarily one-sidedly 'subjectivist' in its compass. On the contrary, governmental action and economic conditions are acknowledged to be important variables which *facilitate* or *constrain* but do not *determine* the processes of decision making within the firm. The 'action' approach is also in principle far more intraorganizational in its compass than a structuralist, politico-economic theory. It infers that general managerial policies and the broader industrial relations climate of the company are likely to be relevant influences. And it acknowledges that the role of other actors (and notably trade unions) may also be germane to understanding the diverse patterns and rates of adoption of profit-sharing and employee-shareholding schemes.

At this point, it is appropriate to analyse empirically the main factors which stimulate the development of employee financial participation in order to appraise these varied positions. The examination commences with an assessment of the role of governments and is followed by an assessment of the 'economic infrastructure' thesis. The ensuing chapters involve a review of the effects of: (1) managerial industrial relations strategies and 'styles'; (2) the industrial relations climate within the company; and (3) employee collectivities (with special reference to the trade unions). A number of interconnections between these sets of variables are also traced that reinforce the central thesis that a *combination* of mutually interacting conditions underlie the spread of economic democracy.

Background

Until approximately two decades ago, British scholars had been traditionally sceptical about the impact of governments in the sphere of industrial relations. Nurtured in a 'tradition of voluntarism', the most commonly held view was that the state should by and large confine its activities to facilitating the processes of collective bargaining between management and trade unions and to ensuring that there was adequate supportive machinery for conciliation, mediation, and arbitration in the event of the parties 'failing to agree'. But direct intervention in industrial relations and, above all, the development of comprehensive labour legislation were seen as unwarranted on two main counts. First, it was argued that such arrangements were unduly cumbersome and ill-adapted to resolving the inevitably diverse range of problems which emanate in particular industrial milieux. And, second, the considered view was that legislation was ineffective. This was partly because of the long-standing distrust of labour courts by trade unionists, but also because employers typically avoided legislative action for fear of sustaining lasting damage to relationships within the firm.

From the end of the 1960s onwards, however, there was a series of changes to voluntarist institutions and the emergence of a far more 'corporatist' industrial relations system. To be sure, the early measures in Britain (such as *In Place of Strife* in 1969 and the Industrial Relations Act 1971) proved to be abortive, but the drift towards state intervention proceeded apace. The thrust of governmental intervention was on the control of pay settlements through various incomes policies and on the regulation of industrial disputes. Moreover, the growing comprehensiveness of state intervention in industrial relations resulted in a series of attempts to enlist the support of trade union officials for overall economic strategy and to secure their involvement in a range of governmental committees.

But the return of a Conservative administration in 1979 heralded a reduction in the influence of some of the existing tripartite machinery and, above all, an avowedly anti-corporatist philosophy so far as economic regulation and industrial relations reform were concerned. None the less, there was no slackening in the policy of relying increasingly on the legislature for the control of trade unions, though the approach adopted in the various Employment and Trade Union Acts was advisedly piecemeal. Moreover, it is clear that these measures have met with considerable success, partly because of the diminished power of trade unions in an era of substantial unemployment, but also because of the new-found willingness of employers to use the legislature to further their industrial relations objectives.

Against such a backcloth, British scholars have begun to recognize that governmental and legislative approaches to employment policy can be highly effective. In legally regulated industrial relations systems (such as in the USA and much of continental Europe) this proposition has of course been accepted for a much longer period. But there is no doubt that governmental legislation in Britain has not only increasingly shaped management–union relations, but has also strongly accelerated the adoption of profit-sharing and share-ownership schemes. Indeed, the evidence clearly reinforces the view that 'external support systems' of this type can appreciably raise the overall level of employee financial participation in a given country. But of course an explanation based on the role of government is less satisfactory in predicting *which* firms will actually adopt schemes.

The USA

In the foregoing chapter it was proposed that the theory of the rise of profit sharing and share ownership based on governmental support was valid for two main types of comparison. Specifically, these were the differences amongst countries at any given point in time, and the changes in a single nation over a period of years. Moreover, there are also grounds for supposing that publicly quoted companies with high capital–labour ratios are favoured by legislation and are thus particularly prone to have adopted share-based schemes.

A theory of cross-national differences in employee financial participation based on the existence of varied legislative supports cannot be empirically assessed in this volume, but it is almost certainly sustainable. Of course there will be many further characteristics of a given country's industrial relations system which will also be relevant to the explanation (the ideologies and values of the parties and their disparate levels of power; managerial policies on this issue; the existing institutions of management–employee relations; and distinctive economic and technological environments) (for reviews of these explanations see IDE 1981a, Hammer and Strauss 1986, Poole 1986a). Yet, as we have already observed, the diverse experiences of West Germany and the USA in particular undoubtedly reflect radically different legislative provisions.

Indeed, the case of the USA is worth mentioning further to show the extent to which Employee Stock-ownership Plans (ESOPs) have been furthered by legislation. ESOPs are currently the most common form of employee ownership in the USA and operate as follows (Rosen *et al.* 1986: 17):

> In an ESOP, the company sets up a special trust, somewhat like an internal bank. It then either contributes cash to buy stock from existing owners, or contributes shares of its own stock. . . . Within limits, the value of these contributions are tax-deductable from the company's income. . . . Stock held in trust is allocated to accounts for individual employees. . . . The stock stays in the trust until the employee leaves the company or retires. Workers acquire a gradually increasing right to the stock in their accounts as they accumulate seniority, a process known as 'vesting'. . . . When employees receive shares, they can hold on to them, sell them to another buyer, or require the company to repurchase them at the fair market price. While the shares are in the trust, the employee pays no tax on them; when they are distributed, the employee has a number of ways to minimize the tax. In family held companies, the value of the stock is determined by an outside appraiser; in publicly traded firms, it is determined by the stock market.

Moreover, these current tax advantages for companies and employees with ESOPs have undoubtedly been the 'primary catalysts for the concept's growth'. As Rosen *et al.* (1986: 15) have documented, in 1974 when Senator Russell Long commenced his activities, there were only about 300 ESOPs in the USA. But by the mid 1980s, as we have seen, there were over 8,000 of these plans in operation.

The British case: a decade of growth

Turning more specifically at this point to the British experience, the view that temporal changes in the spread of employee financial participation are linked with favourable legislation is examined in greater depth and detail. The account begins by a review of the provisions of the various Finance Acts. This is followed by an examination of three main sets of data: (1) official governmental figures on Inland Revenue-approved schemes; (2) a comparison of the situations in 1980 and 1984 based on the Workplace Industrial Relations Survey (WIRS); and (3) information from the Department of Employment survey itself.

The Finance Acts

The modern advance of profit-sharing and share-ownership schemes in Britain can be traced, as we have already noted, to the provisions of the Finance Acts of 1978, 1980, and 1984. There have been a series of modifications to the original proposals (see Deloitte, Haskins, and Sells 1985), but these have not radically altered the underlying tenets of each of the main enactments.

Taking first of all, then, the 1978 Act, the main thrust of this legislation was to stimulate Inland Revenue-approved profit-sharing (APS) schemes. Approval ensured that a series of favourable tax concessions were attracted, being dependent, in turn, upon the schemes meeting various requirements, and notably that they were: (1) administered by trustees; (2) available to all full-time UK employees of a company who have five years' continuous service; (3) based on participation on similar terms (e.g. in relation to pay, on an egalitarian or flat-rate principle, or a weighting for length of service); (4) subject to a maximum value of shares that any one participant may receive in a single year; (5) dependent upon the trustees holding the participant's share for a minimum of two years; (6) founded on a basis whereby dividends paid on shares must be passed on to participants; and (7) based on the principle that shares must be in the company in which the participant works or in a company which controls it. For the participant, the special advantage of APS is that income tax is charged at a marginal rate that is reduced the longer the shares are held in the trust (originally after seven years the percentage of original value charged to income tax was nil; a period which was subsequently reduced to five years).

The 1980 Finance Act covered approved savings-related, share-option schemes and specifically included provision for tax concessions for employee share schemes linked to save as you earn (SAYE) contracts. Again there were several key clauses which have been modified over time, but the main requirements for approval are as follows: (1) shares can only be purchased out of the proceeds of a savings contract specifically designed for this purpose; (2) schemes must be available for all full-time UK employees with at least five years' continuous service (companies can make this qualifying period shorter); (3) participation must be on similar terms for the individuals involved (as under the APS provision); (4) the company can give eligible employees an option to buy the shares in the future at a price not less than 90 per cent of the market value at the time of the grant; (5) the value of the shares on which the option is granted must not exceed the amount repayable from the SAYE contract; (6) there is a specified maximum saving per month (originally £50, which was increased to £100); (7) the option cannot be exercised until the full term of the SAYE contract has expired; and (8) the share must be in the company for which the participant works or a company which controls it.

The third set of provisions were contained in the Finance Act of 1984 and covered *discretionary* and particularly Executive Share-option (ESO) schemes. Under these arrangements, schemes are limited to sections of employees in the firm and, in practice, usually to the senior management of the company. The maximum option that can be granted to an individual was originally proposed at the level of the lesser of four times annual salary or £100,000. The price at which the shares could be acquired was the average market price on the day that they are granted. And normally the option could not be exercised for a minimum of three years. Naturally, these provisions were not designed to increase employee share ownership to the same extent as the 1978 and 1980 Acts; but, as we shall see, they have almost certainly accelerated the growth of ESO schemes in British companies.

Official data based on Inland Revenue submissions and approvals

The passage of these various measures undoubtedly proved to be a strong stimulus to the expansion of profit sharing and share ownership in Britain. Taking first of all the 1978 and 1980 Finance Acts, details of the submissions and approvals to the Inland

Revenue are set out in table 3.1. It will be seen that, up to January 1988, 950 APS schemes had been submitted to the Inland Revenue, of which 711 had been approved; while 811 SAYE schemes had been submitted with 693 receiving approval.

However, this appreciable increase in approved all-employee schemes has not been as spectacular as the expansion of the executive schemes under the 1984 legislation. Indeed, by December 1987, 3,904 ESO schemes had been submitted to and 2,767 approved by the Inland Revenue. To be sure, many of these schemes may have existed before the tax incentives and there-fore the number of submissions to and approvals by the Inland Revenue is no firm indication of the increase in the number of such schemes or their employee coverage. But there can be little doubt that the 1984 Finance Act was conducive to an accelerating development in discretionary share-option schemes in British companies (and that this applies particularly to the ESO variety).

Table 3.1 Cumulative totals of submissions to the Inland Revenue: approved profit-sharing (1978) and save as you earn (1980) schemes

		Finance Act 1978			Finance Act 1980		
		Submitted	Dropped	Approved	Submitted	Dropped	Approved
Up to March	1979	96	–	3	–	–	–
	1980	228	–	117	–	–	–
	1981	327	–	210	82	–	22
	1982	400	–	278	195	–	137
	1983	476	89	344	267	12	215
	1984	552	107	392	362	20	288
	1985	635	116	462	516	27	403
	1986	733	135	532	622	50	514
	1987	845	144	634	728	56	618
Up to Jan	1988	950	163	711	811	71	693

The Workplace Industrial Relations Survey findings

A further means of assessing the growth of profit sharing and employee share ownership in the period since 1978 is from data gathered by the Workplace Industrial Relations Survey (WIRS). This is a nationally representative survey of approximately 2,000 establishments of at least 25 employees. In the report on the 1980 survey (WIRS 1), Daniel and Millward (1983) were able to confirm that share-ownership schemes had indeed become more common since 1978 (roughly 10 per cent of workers in the private sector were by then eligible to participate in such schemes and half of those actually did so) (see Blanchflower and Oswald 1987).

The publication of results from the WIRS 2 survey carried out in

1984 based on a sample of 2,019 establishments indicated a further substantial rise in profit-sharing and share-ownership schemes in the early–mid 1980s (Millward and Stevens 1986). In particular the penetration of share-ownership schemes in industry and commerce would appear to have increased from 13 to 23 per cent of workplaces. And this is certainly suggestive of a boost to employee financial participation arising from the 1980 Finance Act provisions. In more detail, as Millward and Stevens (1986: 259) have documented:

> Schemes remained most common in financial services (69 per cent), although they were already so well established in that sector in 1980 that the rate of increase there was less marked than elsewhere. In retail distribution, which was the next most favoured sector, the proportion rose from 19 per cent to 34 per cent over the four-year period. In 1980, schemes were comparatively rare in manufacturing industry but there has subsequently been growth in that sector too. It was most marked in electrical and instrument engineering, where the incidence has doubled, rising to 32 per cent.
>
> Not only had the number of schemes grown over the period but so also had the coverage of the schemes. Only 15 per cent were for management level only. The proportion of schemes with 100 per cent eligibility rose from 16 per cent to 35 per cent. That doubtless reflected the way in which the new tax exemptions in the 1980 legislation encouraged schemes to be comprehensive in their criteria for eligibility.

The Department of Employment survey (screening phase)

Turning more specifically, then, to the Department of Employment survey reported in this volume and conducted in 1985 by IFF Research Ltd, further estimates can be made of the extent of the various forms of profit sharing and share ownership in contemporary Britain and the role of the legislature as a principal catalyst. In table 3.2 estimates of the penetration of the different types of scheme from the screening phase are presented based on weighted data. It will be seen that over 30 per cent of UK companies have some type of profit-sharing or share-ownership scheme. Moreover, amongst the all-employee schemes, Inland Revenue-approved arrangements dominate in publicly quoted companies (in private companies cash-based profit sharing is the most typical arrangement). The majority of publicly quoted companies have some type of employee financial participation (indeed, only 44 per cent of these firms reported no schemes at all), but schemes are clearly much less common in private companies and in foreign-owned enterprises.

Table 3.2 The penetration of profit-sharing and share-ownership schemes in Britain

Type of scheme	Total	UK publicly quoted companies	UK private companies	Foreign-owned companies
	%	%	%	%
Approved profit sharing (APS)	8	19	2	3
SAYE share option	9	24	2	3
Other share ownership: (all employees)	1	2	0	5
Other share ownership: (selected employees)	11	28	4	3
Cash profit sharing: (all employees)	6	4	7	3
Cash profit sharing: (selected employees)	5	6	5	8
No scheme at all	69	44	81	75

Note: n = 1,125 companies; weighted data.

In table 3.3 further data are presented from the screening phase to provide an estimate of the percentage of companies with any all-employee schemes. Based on weighted data, it would seem that 21 per cent of firms in Britain have one or more of the various types of *all-employee* scheme, with the high level of penetration in publicly quoted companies being again worthy of mention. Variations according to industry type are also evident, with 50 per cent of the firms in the finance sector reporting the presence of one or more of the main all-employee schemes, compared with only 21 per cent in manufacturing and 13 per cent in retail or distribution.

To reinforce the effects of governmental legislation in encouraging the growth of profit sharing and share ownership in modern Britain, it is interesting to note that Inland Revenue-approved schemes would appear to account for 71 per cent of arrangements available to all employees. Measured by 'employees eligible' rather than by companies, the extent of this penetration is of course even more marked. Indeed, on the basis of the screening data obtained by IFF Research Ltd (the survey company) in 1985, over 3.5 million employees in the UK were then eligible for one or other of the main types of scheme. Table 3.4 sets out the data for numbers and percentages of employees eligible and participating

Table 3.3 The extent of profit sharing and share ownership in companies in Britain: all-employee and selected schemes; company ownership; and industry type

	Companies with any all-employee scheme	Companies with selected employee schemes only	Companies with no schemes at all
	%	%	%
Total	21	9	69
Nature of Ownership:			
Publicly quoted	41	14	44
Privately owned	11	7	81
Foreign owned	13	8	79
Industry type:			
Manufacturing	21	10	68
Service	30	14	57
Retail/Distribution	13	7	79
Finance	50	6	44
Other	12	13	75

Notes: Base: all screened companies (n = 1,125).
 Because of rounding not all the figures add up to 100 per cent.

in all-employee schemes. It will be noted that over 2 million employees would appear to be eligible for Inland Revenue-approved SAYE schemes and over 900,000 for APS schemes. Indeed, SAYE schemes were found to be open to approximately three in ten of employees covered in the survey (even though only 8 per cent of all employees would seem actually to participate in them).

Table 3.4 Employee eligibility and participating rates for various types of all-employee profit-sharing and share-ownership schemes

Type of Scheme	Companies		Employees eligible		Employees participating	
	No.	%	No.(000's)	%	No.(000's)	%
Approved profit sharing (APS)	450	8	923	12	689	9
SAYE share option	507	9	2211	29	623	8
Other all-employee share schemes	49	1	99	1	68	1
Cash profit sharing	359	6	293	4	293	4

The Department of Employment survey ('main-stage' and case-study data)

Of course there are companies with arrangements for employee financial participation which preceded the various Finance Acts and which sought Inland Revenue approval for existing schemes when the relevant legislation came into force. However, the dominance of the Inland Revenue-approved schemes cannot be solely explained in this way, not least because, if we examine the timing of introduction of given arrangements, there are no noticeable peaks in the year or two following the passage of legislation. Indeed, as will be seen from table 3.5, based on the 303 'main-stage' firms in which detailed interviews took place, it would appear that only a small minority of approved schemes had been originally introduced prior to the 1978 and 1980 Finance Acts. Moreover, the relatively even pattern of adoption of schemes in the 1980s does suggest a continuing catalytical effect of the legislation on the advance of profit sharing and share ownership in modern Britain.

Table 3.5 Year of introduction of profit-sharing and share-ownership schemes

	APS	SAYE	Other share-based (all-employee) schemes	Cash
Unweighted base:				
all with scheme in question (*n*)	69	116	14	9
	%	%	%	%
1977 or earlier	4	4	41	52
1978	2	1	6	–
1979	16	1	–	16
1980	21	8	–	–
1981	13	15	4	–
1982	10	25	5	–
1983	10	11	23	–
1984	18	25	9	32
1985 (part year)	6	11	12	–

Note: n = 303. The balance of firms had no scheme at all.

The evidence from a variety of sources thus consistently favours the view that the relevant Finance Acts occasioned a sharp and continuing acceleration in the adoption of schemes for employee financial participation in Britain in the 1980s. Of course, as we have argued, the explanation in terms of favourable supporting legislation is most valid for cross-national differences and for the variations over time within a given country. For spatial diversity in a single nation, the supporting role of governments cannot be expected to be a particularly potent explanation. However, further data from the 'main-stage' survey and the case studies undoubtedly suggest that the framing of legislation has particularly favoured the growth of share-based schemes in large-scale publicly quoted companies with high capital–labour ratios.

In the 'main-stage' survey, respondents in companies without schemes were asked whether or not their companies had ever considered introducing schemes and, if so, what the outcome of these deliberations had been. It was found that in 65 per cent of publicly quoted companies without schemes, the managements concerned had never seriously considered introducing schemes. But this percentage was as high as 84 per cent in private firms. Moreover, 25 per cent of the publicly quoted companies without schemes were still considering introducing them, whereas only 11 per cent of private sector firms were in a similar situation.

But the different influences affecting *non*-adoption in companies in the publicly quoted and private sectors were particularly well revealed by the reasons given by key respondents in the 'main-stage' survey for not introducing schemes in the first place. Thus, as is shown in table 3.6, the basic nature of the private company undoubtedly proved the most important single obstacle to profit sharing. And, indeed, respondents typically mentioned the problems of artificial share creation and the lack of a real market value for shares in the private company. By contrast, for the publicly quoted company, an inadequate profits' performance and the characteristics of the workforce were viewed as the main barriers to the adoption of schemes.

Not surprisingly, then, as we have already seen, the penetration of Inland Revenue schemes is most evident amongst publicly quoted companies whose shares have a genuine, and easily realizable, market value. Private companies, by way of contrast, have far greater difficulty in developing arrangements of a share-based type which will obtain Inland Revenue approval. Thus, in the case studies, the company secretary of a small printing and publishing firm without a profit-sharing or employee share-ownership scheme noted:

> The company does not operate any approved or unapproved schemes. The primary reason for this is that we are unquoted which means that there is no market value for our shares, therefore it is virtually impossible to set up a scheme, and to get approval. The company is extremely interested in such schemes and what they entail and has looked at the possibility of such schemes several times in the past. Indeed the company considered this matter usually every 1–2 years. Also the Managing Director is shortly going on a seminar on Share Option schemes. The company's solicitors carried out a lot of

research to try and find a way of introducing a scheme. However, they were not successful. The legislation is too incompatible. The main reason why the company could not set up a scheme to date is thus due to the incompatibilities of the Companies Act and the Finance Acts for setting up the schemes. The latter states that to have share option schemes the shares have to be easily transferable, i.e. to have a market value. However, under the current framework of the company, and within the provisions of the Companies Act, the company has pre-emption clauses on some of its shares, i.e. it distinguishes between different types of shareholders.

Table 3.6 Obstacles to profit-sharing and share-ownership schemes

	Publicly quoted companies (n = 39)	Privately owned firms (n = 43)
Private/family company therefore not appropriate	9	30
Not suitable for our way of working	2	22
No profit available	25	5
Employees would not be interested	14	10
High staff turnover/seasonal workers	16	6
Company in a state of flux	2	5
Too few employees	4	7
Would cost too much to set up	4	4
Policy of good basic pay	2	4
Other	12	6
Ignorance about schemes	11	14

In a private advertising agency, with only an ESO scheme, a not dissimilar argument was put forward:

The company has an ESO scheme and is not in the process of introducing any other schemes. In order to introduce the scheme the company had to alter the company articles, which then had to be circulated to shareholders. This was a major administrative problem. The company has not seriously thought about introducing other schemes, primarily because it is entirely owned by individual shareholders, many of whom are family members, and there is considerable reticence to divide the shareholding. A profit-sharing scheme which paid out on a yearly basis would dilute the shareholding too much in a small company such as this one.

In short, there are substantial difficulties in developing share-based schemes in small private companies which are not quoted on the stock exchange. Indeed, as the first of the two cases above reveals, even in companies in which there is considerable sympathy for profit sharing and share ownership, it is in practice exceedingly difficult to develop schemes. Hence, it is almost certain that the framing of legislation in Britain has been partly responsible for marked differences in adoption rates of profit-sharing and employee-shareholding schemes in publicly quoted and privately owned firms respectively.

Despite some relaxation of the rules in recent years, a further limitation on companies under the existing legislation stems from the role of Investment Protection Committees (IPCs), which are designed to safeguard shareholder interests. These place limits on the share capital which can be issued to employees. In firms with a large capital base these restrictions do not present a major problem, but they can act as a disincentive for firms with a low capital–labour ratio to introduce schemes. This is because, under such circumstances, the value of the shares which may be distributed to individual employees can be too small to act as any appreciable incentive. As the finance director of an oil exploration company observed:

> The main problem with the IPCs is the four times salary
> problem with the parallel option situation. The IPC rules cannot
> be tailormade for each business. The five per cent of issued
> share capital is quite reasonable for us for it is a company with a
> small number of staff and a very large capital base. But, in
> companies with different capital–labour ratios IPCs should be
> more realistic.

Conclusion

In this chapter, it has been established that 'external support' for employee financial participation based on favourable legislation is a principal catalyst for the advancement of schemes. In countries with effective governmental policies for economic democracy there has undoubtedly been a marked growth of profit sharing and share ownership and it is evident that changes over time in a single country are affected by legislation. Moreover, some types of variation in particular nations at a given point in time can also be understood in terms of specific legislative provisions. But given that employee financial participation is still not universally practised, even in countries with supportive legislative provisions, it is clear that other forces must be partially responsible for the considerable spatial differences which remain. In the next four chapters, it will thus be our aim to uncover some of the principal factors which account for the varying patterns of adoption of schemes at a given point in time based on the survey and case-study data from the Department of Employment project itself.

Chapter four

Economic 'infrastructure'

In recent years, increasing attention has focused on materialist theories of relationships at work (Edwards 1986). Modern approaches have been designed as counterpoints to conventional Marxism while, at the same time, disavowing the notions of subjectivity and choice upon which 'action' perspectives are founded. Earlier, non-Marxist materialist interpretations had been discredited by being intimately associated with the idea of convergence (Kerr *et al.* 1960). But partly because of changes in the original assumptions of this particular school (Kerr 1983), and partly because of the appreciation of the considerable variety of economic and technological forms which are evident in similar political systems, a new-found readiness to explore materialist explanations for differences in workplace relationships has latterly emerged.

A theory based on the concept of material 'infrastructure' thus attempts to account for variations in industrial relations phenomena, not by reference to a so-called 'disembodied "structure of norms"' or unrooted "purposive action" but primarily in terms of significant and persistent' disparities in economic and technological conditions (see Ingham 1974: 90). Put simply, differences in, say, the adoption of schemes for employee financial participation would be related to the objective characteristics of companies (e.g. size of organization, growth, and industrial sector) and not to the industrial relations 'styles' of managers or trade unions. Quintessentially, then, this approach is exemplified by model A (set out in chapter 2), in which the development of profit sharing and share ownership is traced to the external forces of government action and economic 'infrastructure' that determine outcomes irrespective of the choices of those actually involved in the processes of organizational decision making itself. To be sure, some modern materialist approaches (and notably that espoused by Edwards (1986)) are essentially intraorganizational in compass. But they all

53

involve the rejection of subjectivity (and particularly of strategic choices) in accounting for observable variations from one firm to the next.

At this point, these arguments are assessed in relation to the empirical evidence. In the survey and case-study phases of the Department of Employment research, it was only possible to examine the effects of a number of economic variables and not a wider range of 'material' conditions (including technology). The data are sufficient, however, to show that certain characteristics of companies are related to the propensity of firms to adopt profit-sharing and share-ownership schemes. However, they also suggest that only part of the variance can be explained on the basis of these assumptions alone. As we shall see, therefore, a more comprehensive explanation must incorporate a variety of subjective and institutional factors exemplified by model B and encapsulated in the 'action' approach.

Survey data

In chapter 3, evidence of the effects of a given firm being publicly quoted on the stock exchange upon the development of share-based schemes for employee financial participation was presented. As we observed, this relationship has depended in part upon the framing of governmental legislation; but it is also integral to the structure of companies. After all, it is obvious that, in firms in which shares are issued, it is far easier to develop schemes compared with small-scale private concerns where only cash-based profit sharing may be feasible. In the previous chapter, we also highlighted the consequences of capital–labour ratio for the growth of share-based schemes under current Investment Protection Committee guidelines. The economic 'infrastructure' thesis is now examined in further detail by reference to data on the effects of: (1) enterprise size; (2) diverse rates of growth of particular companies; and (3) industrial sector.

The fieldwork in the survey stage of the research involved interviewing one key management respondent in each company (usually the company secretary). In the first instance this comprised a short telephoning screening interview in 1,125 companies in order to obtain information on the extent of profit-sharing and share-ownership arrangements and to provide a sample for the 'main-stage' survey. The more detailed interviews which followed covered 303 companies and, in these, it was possible to explore the reasons for the adoption or non-adoption of particular arrangements and to obtain more comprehensive information on the companies themselves. The survey data presented in chapter 3 were largely based on the screening interviews. The information which is now examined is appropriately from the 'main-stage' survey and facilitates a more rigorous statistical analysis of the factors which affect the varied rates of adoption of profit-sharing and employee-shareholding schemes in contemporary Britain.

Enterprise size

To assess the effects of enterprise size on the propensity of firms to develop one or other of the various arrangements for employee financial participation, information is presented on capital assets, annual turnover, multi- or single establishment, and company autonomy. The tables are designed to accommodate four main situations in the enterprise, covering the cases of the adoption of: (1) any general (i.e. all-employee) scheme; (2) any scheme (including those with only a partial coverage of employees); (3) Inland Revenue-approved profit-sharing (APS) schemes; and (4) Inland Revenue-approved save as you earn (SAYE) share-option schemes. In detail, the heading 'any general scheme' covers both approved and non-approved arrangements, and cash-based as well as share-based profit sharing. The main criterion of inclusion is that the firms concerned had to have at least *one* type of scheme that in principle applied to all of its employees. The category 'any scheme' includes all the firms under the heading 'any general scheme' and companies with *discretionary* schemes (whether approved or non-approved). The APS and SAYE cases are obviously more limited cases. The firm concerned had to have that specific type of Inland Revenue-approved scheme to be included (though some of these firms obviously had more than one type of scheme).

Of all the structural characteristics of companies examined in this study, capital assets and annual turnover were found to be the most important explanatory variables. Indeed, there is clear evidence that larger-scale, capital-intensive enterprises with a substantial annual turnover are particularly likely to have adopted profit-sharing and share-ownership schemes. The capital assets of companies were measured in the following bands: £1m and under; £1–£3.5m; £3.5–£10m; £10–£50m; and £50m and over. In table 4.1, the relevant data are presented. It will be seen that whereas small concerns (with capital assets of £1m and under) are unlikely to have schemes, almost all the largest firms (with assets of £50m or over) have adopted one or more of the generally based programmes. Although the relationship remains strong (Cramer's *V*

The origins of economic democracy

= 0.31, $p \leqslant 0.001$), the effects of capital assets are least pronounced for the APS schemes. Moreover, as we shall see, these differences are partly explicable by the propensity of finance sector companies to have developed APS schemes regardless of the size of the firm itself.

Turning to the annual turnover of companies, this was assessed on the basis of nine different bands (under £1m; £1–£3.5m; £3.5–£10m; £11–£49m; £50–£99m; £100–£199m; £200–£499m; £500–£999m; and £1,000m or more). It will be seen from table 4.2 that firms with an annual turnover of £500m or more are particularly likely to have a generally based scheme for employee financial participation. This applies particularly to the SAYE schemes (Cramer's $V = 0.56$, $p \leqslant 0.0001$). Nevertheless, there is an exception in the case of APS schemes where annual turnover is not significant. Once again the reasons for this difference are almost certainly related to the fact that financial sector firms are so likely to adopt these profit-sharing schemes that this would appear to occur largely irrespective of annual financial performance of the company.

Whether or not a company is a single- or multi-establishment firm is also of course linked to enterprise size. As is to be expected from the trend in the evidence examined so far, multi- rather than single-establishment enterprises are thus likely to have adopted generally based (i.e. all-employee) schemes for profit sharing and share ownership (see table 4.3). Once again, however, these effects do not apply for the APS schemes.

Of further interest is to discover to what extent the *autonomy* of managements to make decisions independently of their head offices is related to employee financial participation. Respondents were thus asked how much autonomy each establishment had in this respect ranging from *no autonomy* (all decisions on the introduction of schemes centralized/taken at head office), through *some autonomy* (e.g. can initiate schemes but have to submit proposals for approval), to *complete autonomy* (no authorization needed from head office). However, as is revealed in table 4.3, autonomy of establishment is not significantly related to the varied patterns of adoption of the main types of profit-sharing and share-ownership schemes in companies in Britain.

Company growth

The economic 'infrastructure' thesis is based on the assumption of considerable dynamism in the material base of given societies at specific points in time. More specifically, it recognizes that,

Table 4.1 Capital assets of companies and profit sharing or share ownership (n = 264)

Capital assets	General scheme		Any scheme		Inland Revenue-approved profit-sharing (APS) scheme		Inland Revenue-approved save as you earn (SAYE) scheme	
	Yes	No	Yes	No	Yes	No	Yes	No
£1m and under	3	18	5	16	0	21	0	21
£1–£3.5m	13	17	17	13	4	26	2	28
£3.5–£10m	30	25	37	18	7	48	18	37
£10–£50m	40	19	48	11	12	47	28	31
£50m and over	88	11	93	6	39	60	62	37
Totals	174	90	200	64	62	202	110	154

Notes: For general scheme: chi-square = 58.2 (degrees of freedom = 4), significance = 0.001, Cramer's V = 0.47.
For any scheme: chi-square = 57.8 (degrees of freedom = 4), significance = 0.001, Cramer's V = 0.47.
For Inland Revenue-approved profit-sharing (APS) scheme: chi-square = 26.0 (degrees of freedom = 4), significance = 0.001, Cramer's V = 0.31.
For Inland Revenue-approved save as you earn (SAYE) scheme: chi-square = 50.6 (degrees of freedom = 4), significance = 0.001, Cramer's V = 0.44.

Table 4.2 Annual turnover of companies and profit sharing or share ownership (*n* = 289)

Annual turnover	General scheme		Any scheme		Inland Revenue-approved profit-sharing (APS) scheme		Inland Revenue-approved save as you earn (SAYE) scheme	
	Yes	*No*	*Yes*	*No*	*Yes*	*No*	*Yes*	*No*
Under £1m	1	2	1	2	0	3	0	3
£1–£3.5m	7	6	8	5	1	12	1	12
£3.5–£10m	23	30	28	25	10	43	5	48
£11–£49m	43	43	53	33	15	71	21	65
£50–£99m	22	11	27	6	20	23	12	21
£100–£199m	25	8	31	2	6	27	20	13
£200–£499m	21	4	22	3	9	16	17	8
£500–£999m	15	0	15	0	3	12	15	0
£1,000m or more	26	2	26	2	10	18	22	6
Totals	183	106	211	78	74	225	113	176

Notes: For general scheme: chi-square = 43.5 (degrees of freedom = 8), significance = 0.001, Cramer's *V* = 0.39.
For any scheme: chi-square = 42.5 (degrees of freedom = 8), significance = 0.001, Cramer's *V* = 0.38.
For Inland Revenue-approved profit-sharing (APS) scheme: not significant.
For Inland Revenue-approved save as you earn (SAYE) scheme: chi-square = 91.7 (degrees of freedom = 8), significance = 0.0001, Cramer's *V* = 0.56.

Table 4.3 Multi- or single establishment, autonomy, and profit sharing or share ownership

Multi- or single establishment	General scheme (n = 303)		Any scheme (n = 303)		Inland Revenue-approved profit-sharing (APS) scheme (n = 303)		Inland Revenue-approved save as you earn (SAYE) scheme (n = 303)	
	Yes	No	Yes	No	Yes	No	Yes	No
Multi-establishment	171	78	196	53	59	190	116	133
Single establishment	20	34	25	29	10	44	4	50
Totals	191	112	221	82	69	234	120	183
Autonomy	(n = 241)		(n = 241)		(n = 241)		(n = 241)	
No autonomy	138	56	155	39	51	143	95	99
Some autonomy	25	15	32	8	5	35	16	24
Complete autonomy	4	3	5	2	2	5	0	7
Totals	167	74	192	49	58	183	111	130

Notes: For general scheme: (1) multi- or single establishment: chi-square = 17.7 (degrees of freedom = 1), significance = 0.001, Cramer's V = 0.25; (2) autonomy not significant.
For any scheme: (1) multi- or single establishment: chi-square = 22.0 (degrees of freedom = 1), significance = 0.001, Cramer's V = 0.28; (2) autonomy not significant.
For Inland Revenue-approved profit-sharing (APS) scheme: multi- or single establishment and autonomy not significant.
For Inland Revenue-approved save as you earn (SAYE) scheme: (1) multi- or single establishment: chi-square = 26.9 (degrees of freedom = 1), significance = 0.0001, ϕ = 0.31; (2) autonomy: chi-square = 7.2 (degrees of freedom = 2), significance = 0.03, Cramer's V = 0.17.

whereas some companies may be growing appreciably and experiencing tight labour market conditions, others will be in terminal decline with employee financial participation appearing to be largely an irrelevant issue. These arguments are further linked with the notions of labour market segmentation and the diverse experiences of firms undergoing rapid technological change that were also featured in chapter 2.

To assess the effects of company growth on the adoption of profit-sharing and share-ownership schemes respondents were asked on identical three-point scales whether, in terms of its activities in the last five years, the organization had experienced: (1) an increase; (2) stayed the same; or (3) a decrease. The results are set out in table 4.4, where it will be seen that, for the most part, trends in the workforce are *not* significantly related to the experience of profit sharing and share ownership (the one exception being for the APS schemes). By contrast, there are pronounced effects of trends in business volume for the introduction of all schemes except the SAYE type. But, there is clearly no *automatic* tendency for a rise in business volume to be accompanied by an expansion in the workforce and for both to be related to an increased propensity to introduce profit-sharing or share-ownership schemes.

The probable explanations for this pattern of results are as follows. In firms with an expanding workforce, APS schemes are particularly valuable for furthering the goal of staff retention. However, SAYE schemes require a positive commitment on the part of the employee to participate and thus, from a management standpoint, they do not provide the same potential incentive for the employee to remain in the firm. Hence APS schemes are preferred to SAYE schemes by managements in expanding businesses. Moreover, the lack of any direct link between the effects of a growing workforce and business volume may be because employers have increasingly preferred to substitute capital for labour in conditions of economic growth. And, at all events, the data reveal the limitations of the economic 'infrastructure' thesis so far as the predicted consequences of company expansion for profit sharing and share ownership are concerned, not least because the relationships which do obtain appear to reflect distinctive managerial policies and strategies, rather than the direct determining consequences of material forces themselves.

Industrial sector

On the basis of the data presented in chapter 3 from the screening interviews, it has already been shown that the development of

Table 4.4 Trends in the workforce and in business volume and profit sharing or share ownership

Trends in the workforce	General scheme (n = 299)		Any scheme (n = 299)		Inland Revenue-approved profit-sharing (APS) scheme (n = 299)		Inland Revenue-approved save as you earn (SAYE) scheme (n = 299)	
	Yes	No	Yes	No	Yes	No	Yes	No
Increased	87	42	100	29	41	88	49	80
Decreased	78	51	92	37	19	110	54	75
Stayed the same	23	18	25	16	8	33	14	27
Totals	188	111	217	82	68	231	117	182
Trends in business volume	(n = 292)		(n = 292)		(n = 292)		(n = 292)	
Increased	149	66	168	47	59	156	90	125
Decreased	19	21	23	17	3	37	16	24
Stayed the same	15	22	20	17	4	33	8	29
Totals	183	109	211	81	66	226	114	178

Notes: For general scheme: (1) trends in the workforce not significant; (2) trends in business volume: chi-square = 15.7 (degrees of freedom = 2), significance = 0.001, Cramer's V = 0.23.
For any scheme: (1) trends in the workforce not significant; (2) trends in business volume: chi-square = 14.2 (degrees of freedom = 2), significance = 0.001, Cramer's V = 0.22.
For Inland Revenue-approved profit-sharing (APS) scheme: (1) trends in the workforce: chi-square = 11.0 (degrees of freedom = 2), significance = 0.004, Cramer's V = 0.19; (2) trends in business volume: chi-square = 11.0 (degrees of freedom = 2), significance = 0.004, Cramer's V = 0.19.
For Inland Revenue-approved save as you earn (SAYE) scheme: trends in workforce and in business volume not significant.

profit sharing and share ownership for employees varies according to industrial sector, with financial-type companies being the most likely to have adopted schemes. Further corroborative evidence based on the 'main-stage' survey is set out in table 4.5, which reveals the relationship between primary business activity of the company (manufacturing, services, retail/distribution, finance, and other) and the adoption of one or other of the main forms of employee financial participation. It will be noted that almost all the firms in the finance sector have some form of generally based scheme for profit sharing or share ownership, even though this is practised by only a minority of service sector companies. Moreover, the effects of industrial sector are particularly pronounced for APS schemes. Thus, no less than half of the finance sector firms have APS arrangements compared with only one-sixth of their counterparts in manufacturing.

More generally, then, the economic 'infrastructure' thesis is supported by the effects of the industrial sector. Nevertheless, as we shall see, the case studies revealed that objective structural factors (associated with the location of the firm in a particular part of the economy) are undoubtedly affected by differences in managerial objectives and policies on employee relations. Moreover, the fact that, even in the financial sector, some firms do *not* have all-employee schemes (and several have not adopted the more specific APS variety) suggests that the structural location of a company is by no means a determinant of outcomes. Indeed, there would still appear to be a substantial measure of choice in the selection of actual arrangements amongst the key decision makers in the companies.

The *case studies* thus enabled further information to be brought to bear to explain the findings of the survey. Indeed, on the basis of these data, it would seem that there are at least four main reasons for the intersector differences: (1) competitive labour market conditions; (2) the profitability of financial sector firms; (3) characteristics of employees; and (4) knowledge and information on schemes.

More specifically, then, financial sector firms are particularly likely to introduce schemes (and particularly the APS type) because they are the most prone to experience competition in attracting and retaining staff. As a company secretary in a large finance sector firm pointed out: 'Employee benefits of this kind were being offered in the financial sector and the company felt it should offer these schemes to its employees in order to remain competitive with other financial sector companies.'

Moreover, at least one of our finance sector firms had changed

Table 4.5 Primary business activity and profit sharing or share ownership (n = 303)

Primary business activity	General scheme (i.e. applying to whole workforce)		Any scheme		Inland Revenue-approved profit-sharing (APS) scheme		Inland Revenue-approved save as you earn (SAYE) scheme	
	Yes	No	Yes	No	Yes	No	Yes	No
Manufacturing	91	46	106	31	19	118	65	72
Services	15	17	19	13	6	26	10	22
Retail/distribution	30	29	36	23	14	45	18	41
Finance	42	8	45	5	25	25	21	29
Other	13	12	15	10	5	20	6	19
Totals	191	112	221	82	69	234	120	183

Notes: For general scheme: chi-square = 18.8 (degrees of freedom = 4), significant at 0.001 level, Cramer's V = 0.25.
For any scheme: chi-square = 18.1 (degrees of freedom = 4), significant at 0.01 level, Cramer's V = 0.24.
For Inland Revenue-approved profit-sharing (APS) scheme: chi-square = 27.7 (degrees of freedom = 4), significant at 0.001 level, Cramer's V = 0.30.
For Inland Revenue-approved save as you earn (SAYE) scheme: chi-square = 10.3 (degrees of freedom = 4), significant at 0.05 level, Cramer's V = 0.17.

the eligibility criterion for its SAYE scheme because of concern over labour turnover and staff pressure, as the company secretary recalled:

> The original eligibility criterion for the scheme was three years continuous full-time service. This was because it was felt that the scheme should be offered to long-serving staff as a form of reward for their loyalty to the company. However, in 1982–3 the criterion was lowered to one year's continuous full-time service or at least three years continuous part-time service (where part-time service means being in employment for at least twenty hours a week). In a general sense the company decided on this because an increase in labour turnover seemed to warrant it, but secondly the suggestion arose from staff committees, and it was in response to those suggestions.

Most finance sector firms have also been able to maintain relatively high levels of profit even in a period of recession (and, as we have seen, firms with high levels of turnover and an expanding business volume are particularly likely to have all-employee schemes). Moreover, in financial sector firms, managements have a greater knowledge and appreciation of the tax and other advantages of introducing schemes. For instance, as the company secretary of a finance sector firm pointed out: 'There was no particular source of knowledge about the schemes. This company is in the insurance and finance business and hence has always had a general knowledge of such schemes.'

Relative importance of the variables

Before developing a more detailed critique of one-sidedly materialist explanations for the rise of profit-sharing and share-ownership schemes, it is worth exploring in greater depth the relative saliency of the main variables which have been isolated in this chapter. Again the analysis applies to the four cases of the adoption in companies of any all-employee scheme, any scheme, APS schemes, and SAYE schemes.

In table 4.6 data are presented based on the correlation co-efficients between a series of enterprise characteristics and whether or not the companies concerned had introduced the various forms of profit sharing or employee share ownership. For the categories of any general scheme and any scheme the results are almost identical. It will be seen that the presence of higher rather than lower capital assets is the strongest single predictor of the adoption of schemes. This is followed by annual turnover in the company,

Table 4.6 The existence of various schemes for profit sharing and groups of explanatory variables based on the economic 'infrastructure' thesis (**Pearson product moment correlation coefficients**)

Explanatory variables (company characteristics)	General scheme	Any scheme (including 1984 Act provisions)	Inland Revenue-approved profit-sharing (APS) scheme	Inland Revenue-approved save as you earn (SAYE) scheme
Higher rather than lower capital assets	0.42[a]	0.37[a]	0.29[a]	0.39[a]
Higher rather than lower annual turnover	0.37[a]	0.34[a]	0.15[a]	0.54[a]
Multi- rather than single establishment	0.25[a]	0.27[a]	0.05	0.31[a]
Higher rather than lower extent of establishment autonomy	0.09	-0.02	-0.05	-0.15[b]
Extent of increase in workforce	0.07	0.06	0.19[a]	-0.01
Extent of increase in business volume	0.20[a]	0.20[a]	0.19[a]	0.13[c]
Enterprise in financial sector	0.19[a]	0.17[a]	0.29[a]	0.02

Notes: [a] significant at 0.001 level; [b] significant at 0.01 level; [c] significant at 0.05 level. The numbers range between 137 and 303.

multi- rather than single establishment, trends in business volume, and the enterprise being in the financial sector (in all cases, the relationships are significant at the $p < 0.001$ level). It will also be noted that establishment autonomy and trends in the workforce are irrelevant to the explanation.

For the more specific case of the presence of APS schemes in the company, however, a rather different pattern of relationships is discernible. The location of the firm in the financial sector is particularly important as a predictor (this variable is no less salient than capital assets in accounting for the adoption of this specific form of employee financial participation). Trends in the workforce and in business volume are both highly significant ($p = 0.001$). By contrast, the relationship between company turnover levels and the adoption of APS schemes is weak, and there are no effects whatsoever of the firm being a multi- rather than single establishment and of establishment autonomy.

Finally, the variables linked with the different degrees of penetration of SAYE schemes are again distinctive. Company turnover is by far the most important predictor of the adoption of schemes ($r = 0.54$, $p < 0.0001$), followed by the capital assets of the company, and whether or not the firm concerned is multi- or single establishment. None of the other explanatory variables is of major consequence and indeed, as we have seen, the location of the firm in the financial sector is largely irrelevant to the adoption of SAYE schemes.

Conclusions

The patterning of the data revealed in this chapter is thus important in two main respects. First, it demonstrates the existence of a highly complex phenomenon and the necessity of disaggregating the dependent variable if an adequate understanding of the rise of profit-sharing and share-ownership schemes in Britain is to occur. The thrust of the economic 'infrastructure' thesis (that large firms in the financial sector experiencing an increase in the workforce and in business volume are particularly likely to develop employee financial participation) applies most obviously to the APS schemes. But even in these cases it is clear that only part of the variance can be accounted for on the basis of this group of variables. And, second, it clarifies the argument that the effects of the main enterprise characteristics are in turn highly diverse (and not always *structurally* consistent). This further suggests that there are substantial mediating influences to be discovered that relate to the choices of those actually involved in deciding whether or not to introduce profit sharing and share ownership for employees in the first place.

Chapter five

Managerial strategies and 'styles'

From the arguments presented so far in this monograph it will be
evident that a comprehensive explanation for the rise of profit
sharing and share ownership must encompass the perceptions of
the initiators of the schemes themselves. Facilitative legislation is
an invaluable incentive for companies to promote employee
financial participation, while the economic performance of a firm
does affect the decision on whether or not to develop profit
sharing. But these are not sufficient conditions. The tax advantages which stem from Inland Revenue approval apply to all large,
British, publicly quoted enterprises, but by no means every firm
has adopted a scheme. Moreover, only some companies in a
healthy financial position have used this favourable bedrock to
advance employee involvement in ownership. The motives and
objectives of the key personnel in the enterprise are thus of far
reaching consequence for understanding the diverse modes of
adoption of schemes in Britain as well.

In this chapter, these arguments are pursued by way of an
analysis of the perceptions of managers who are either responsible
for, or heavily implicated in, their firm's schemes. To commence
with these personnel is entirely appropriate because initial discussions on profit sharing and share ownership are typically confined
to management. Thus, on the basis of the findings from the 'main-
stage' survey, in only one in five cases where an APS or SAYE
scheme was under consideration were the employees themselves
found to be involved in the decision to have a scheme. Moreover,
in 90 per cent of firms setting up schemes, decisions regarding the
type of scheme chosen and on the rules governing eligibility were
taken by management alone.

Managerial strategies and objectives

To assess managerial perceptions in more detail, an examination is
conducted of actual objectives in introducing schemes. Findings
from the survey are enriched by case-study data to provide

additional insights into strategic thinking in this respect. The relationships between objectives and functional specialisms within management and the timing of the introduction of schemes are then examined. The link between management 'styles' in industrial relations and the diverse patterns of adoption of profit sharing and share ownership in firms in Britain is also demonstrated.

Survey data

In the 'main-stage' survey, key managerial respondents were asked to attribute relative importance to a set of different objectives rated on five-point scales, where 1 signified 'not at all important' and 5 'very important'. The mean scores from these ratings are set out in table 5.1. It will be seen that the objectives which feature the most prominently are those of making employees: (1) feel they are part of the company; and (2) more profit conscious. The aims of increasing the sense of commitment to the company and of ensuring that employees benefit from company profitability are also of major importance. However, the advantages of profit sharing as a tax-efficient means of reward for the company and as a means of holding wage claims down are of limited relevance in shaping managerial strategies.

Information was also elicited in a more open-ended way from respondents on the factors leading to the actual adoption of various forms of profit sharing and share ownership. As is shown in table 5.2, the dominant motives appeared to be the desire of companies: (1) to make staff feel more involved or interested; (2) to reward staff in an efficient way; (3) to reward or benefit staff; and (4) to keep up with other companies. Is is also evident that different factors appeared to underlie the main types of scheme, with the aim of making the staff feel more involved or interested applying particularly to APS schemes, while that of rewarding or benefiting the staff being particularly common for cash profit-sharing arrangements.

Case-study data

In the survey stage of the research, some interesting pointers to managerial objectives in adopting schemes thus emerged. In the case studies, managerial objectives in introducing schemes were examined in greater depth and, indeed, a complex of partly distinctive and partly intertwined aims were discovered. Even in the same company, different managerial personnel emphasized rather disparate (though not necessarily competing) objectives.

Table 5.1 Objectives of schemes as assessed by key respondents in the 'main-stage' survey

Objectives	APS	SAYE	Other scheme	Cash
To make employees feel they are part of the company	4.5	4.4	4.1	4.3
To make employees more profit conscious	4.3	4.2	3.9	4.6
To increase sense of commitment to the company	4.0	3.9	4.3	4.1
To ensure that employees benefit from company profitability	3.9	3.6	3.6	4.3
Tax-efficient means of reward for employees	3.7	3.6	–	–
Incentive for greater productivity	3.4	2.9	3.1	3.7
To increase sense of co-operation between management and the workforce	3.2	3.2	2.8	3.8
To increase employees' understanding of financial issues	2.9	3.0	2.2	3.4
Tax-efficient means of reward for company	2.8	2.0	–	–
To help hold wage claims down	1.4	1.1	1.1	1.8
Number of schemes	69	116	14	31

Table 5.2 Factors leading to the introduction of schemes

Company wanted . . .	APS	SAYE	Other all-employee share scheme	Cash profit sharing
	%	%	%	%
To make staff feel more involved/interested	51	35	41	–
Tax-efficient way of rewarding staff	15	10	–	5
To reward/benefit staff	14	16	15	48
To keep up with other companies/part of the general climate	14	13	–	–
Had been discussing it for years and finally did it	10	5	–	21
To encourage staff loyalty	9	1	–	–
To make employees feel that they have a say	7	4	17	6
To increase productivity	5	1	–	18
Number of schemes	69	116	14	9

Clearly to make sense of these elements requires classification with five main factors being uppermost in the case-study interviews.

The origins of economic democracy

(1) Moral commitment

This applied particularly to some of the earliest non-approved schemes in companies. In these cases, a senior management group (and not infrequently the founder of the firm) had a moral commitment to involving employees in the ownership of the company. The motivation here was highly principled and sometimes entailed a coherent strategy for the sharing of gain, knowledge, and power. In one company, for instance, the founder saw employee share-holding and profit sharing as an extension of a strongly held political philosophy and this led him to 'want people who worked for the company to feel part of it'. This also affected practice because the objective in the earliest days was that *everyone* should benefit from the success of the company and that no one should be excluded on the criterion of hours worked per week. In short, part-timers were deliberately included in the scheme from the outset.

(2) Staff retention

However, in the case studies (and in particular in companies with fully approved schemes), a calculative form of paternalism was empirically more common. The objective here was to encourage employees to feel part of the company and to increase the likelihood of their *remaining* members. But, in contrast with the moral commitment of type (1), emphasis was placed on the commercial and competitive advantages of such a policy. This applied particularly to firms in the finance sector where competition in the labour market for able personnel has remained acute. Comments from key respondents under this heading included 'to reward and keep the company staff' and 'to reward the loyal staff'.

(3) Employee involvement

We shall explore the links between profit sharing and share ownership and employee involvement at greater length in chapter 6. It is clear, however, that a common objective in introducing schemes was to increase employee involvement in the company. In a manufacturing firm, for instance, it was argued that 'each employee had a right to part of the company', while in a service sector firm it was suggested that a principal objective 'was to promote financial participation in the company. This fits in with the participatory methods of management in the company, which involves widespread consultation with the employees.'

A related objective was to increase the employee's sense of ownership. This is, of course, linked with wider ideologically based conceptions of a property-owning democracy though it was seldom articulated in precisely these terms. However, some key respondents noted that these schemes are a long-run incentive and *are* distinct from bonuses and other variable forms of remuneration precisely because they can inculcate an ownership consciousness. And indeed, one manager specifically noted that share-ownership schemes can increase the feelings of identity of employees with shareholder interests.

Involvement through share schemes was also related to the desire to encourage a commercial awareness on the part of employees. Indeed, it was not uncommon for respondents to note the advantages of increased commercial understanding, identifying a greater willingness to consult the financial pages of newspapers and being aware of the costs involved in inefficiency and waste.

Again, a not untypical objective was the desire to motivate employees. Probing respondents on this item frequently led to the acknowledgement that the links between profit sharing and share ownership and motivation to work were distant and tenuous. But a number of managers still stressed such a concern. For instance, the group secretary of a financial sector company noted that 'it was hoped that schemes would motivate staff in the business and link profits with performance'. And this sentiment was echoed by the company secretary of another firm in the financial sector who argued that: 'as a general principle it was felt that it would be beneficial to the company through increasing employee awareness of the company, therefore, their incentive to work hard, hence increasing profits and share price'.

(4) Improved industrial relations performance

Another rationale for introducing schemes was to improve relations between company and employees. Again our probes revealed that many respondents felt such a relationship was distant. But, in a unionized manufacturing firm, it was certainly noted that there were disadvantages in industrial relations terms of *not* introducing schemes. Indeed, 'good' employers were seen as developing profit sharing and share ownership because of the internal opposition and *disincentive* effects of making substantial profits without any compensatory rewards for employees.

(5) Protection against takeover

Some managers in the case studies also considered that there were potential advantages of employee share ownership in the event of merger/takeover. Indeed, if a firm was potentially vulnerable to takeover, employee shareholding was seen as a potentially useful counter-measure (and especially when shares were held in trust). One or two cases were cited of takeovers being successfully deterred in this way. Moreover, some firms sought a relaxation of Investment Protection Committee rulings on employee shareholding to enable them to 'ward off' predatorial companies.

Sometimes, however, the case was argued very differently but still in an advantageous way for the development of employee shareholding. Thus in some firms which were *active in taking over other companies*, it was argued that profit-sharing and share-ownership schemes could defuse the issue by allaying the fears of employees in firms which were being absorbed into the new group. This arises because the company can point to its own advanced employee involvement practices which will be developed throughout the new group.

Managerial objectives and functional specialisms

Managerial objectives in introducing profit-sharing and share-ownership schemes are thus complex and are exacerbated by the functional separation of managerial activities in all but the smallest of firms. To some extent, of course, all managers are involved in industrial relations, but the specialist handling of pay negotiations and the formulation of industrial relations policies are likely to be within the specialist province of personnel departments. However, the technicalities of legislation on profit sharing and share ownership and the detailed handling of individual cases are more suited to the finance rather than the personnel function. There is some evidence, too, that these functional differences are reflected in diverse managerial attitudes to employee financial participation. To be sure, in case studies, it is difficult to quantify these differences. But while almost all the managers were found to be broadly supportive to such developments, the greatest enthusiasm and commitment was found amongst company secretaries and financial directors. Their colleagues in personnel (while again being typically favourable to these schemes) tended to consider that the impact upon employees was likely to be circumscribed and they were much more committed to operating conventional collective bargaining.

Timing of introduction of schemes

The *timing* of introduction of schemes and the differences between companies which embarked upon schemes early on and those which have only recently introduced them are linked with diverse managerial objectives. Following our case-study discussions with key respondents, it was considered important to distinguish between three types here: (1) very early schemes pre-dating recent legislation; (2) schemes introduced in the late 1970s and early 1980s; and (3) the recent period of the mid 1980s. Before analysing these rather different situations, however, it should be mentioned that we detected in firms a broad *evolutionary* trend towards introducing *more* types of scheme. This applied particularly to ESO schemes which are very likely to have been introduced in the eighteen months–two years following on from the provisions of the 1984 Act.

In general, however, there *are* variations in objectives and patterns of employee–management relations linked with the question of timing. The very earliest schemes almost inevitably reflect the distinctive values of top management. In particular, there is in such concerns a feeling of moral commitment on the part of management to profit sharing. This applies particularly to the earliest non-approved schemes, and, indeed, their introduction is typically accompanied by a statement of company philosophy in this respect. In one case, the impetus did come from employee representatives through a staff association, but it was far more common for the decision to stem from upper echelons within management. To be sure, some early non-approved schemes ultimately received Inland Revenue approval but their *genesis* belongs to this earlier period. And, of course, some of the early models were influential in the framing of modern legislation and hence are by no means incompatible with it.

The next wave of advance followed on from the 1978 and 1980 Acts. The underlying managerial rationale appears to have been typically one of either 'staff attraction and retention' or 'employee involvement'. As we have seen, a number of firms, particularly in the finance sector and experiencing tight labour market constraints, undoubtedly view APS schemes as a valuable inducement for attracting and retaining high-calibre staff. And others, broadly committed to the goal of involving employees in the company, see SAYE schemes as an inexpensive way of furthering this goal. Moreover, these types of company were the ones which were typically at the forefront of the late 1970s and early 1980s expansion.

Apart from the *evolutionary* factor which explains *some* recent schemes (and particularly again the development of the ESO type), late introduction is usually associated with perceived pressure from competitors. Again this applies above all to finance sector firms where some managements, regardless of industrial style and views on employee involvement, clearly feel compelled to introduce schemes because competitive companies have flourishing arrangements. Further factors associated with late introduction are the increased interest in these schemes in Britain in the 1980s and, less commonly, the delaying effect of a degree of union opposition to APS-type schemes. In particular, in one manufacturing firm, there was hostility to a share-based proposal, and it therefore took the company much longer to introduce a planned scheme than it had intended. Finally, there is a preference for introducing schemes against a background of rising profitability and turnover and hence there were cases of delayed adoption because of an indifferent company economic performance when the idea was first being seriously discussed.

Managerial 'styles' in industrial relations

The potential importance of managerial 'styles' in industrial relations for the development of profit sharing and share ownership was emphasized in chapter 2. For empirical purposes, the most fruitful way to proceed appeared to be to concentrate on developing measures of the consultative and paternal 'styles', since there are sound reasons to suppose that these should be linked with the growth on profit sharing and share ownership. A series of questions in the 'main-stage' survey were thus designed to assess these two industrial relations 'styles'. Respondents in each company were asked (on five-point scales from very appropriate to not at all appropriate) whether or not a series of policies were practised in their companies. For the consultative 'style', the items included: (1) to involve employees in full partnership with management to serve the overall objectives of the company as a whole; (2) to inform employees or their representatives on a regular basis about company objectives and day-to-day management; and (3) to accept that most employees are committed to their unions and hence to encourage collective bargaining on a regular basis. The first two focused on general policies on employee involvement and information sharing which are arguably basic to the consultative 'style'. The third involved countenancing the possibility of managements *also* encouraging trade union types of involvement alongside employee-centred forms (see Brown and Sisson 1984). The items in the paternal 'style' covered: (1) to expect loyalty from employees in return for an advanced welfare package; (2) to encourage employees to fulfil their maximum potential; and (3) to consider the company's obligations to the workforce are confined only to working hours. Again, for the first two measures, the focus on loyalty and human-resource development were viewed as important elements of the paternal 'style'. For balance, the third item was constructed in anticipation of a negative response (i.e. paternalist managers were seen as likely to reject the view that a company's obligations to employees are confined only to working hours).

The provenance of the measures of the consultative and paternal 'styles' was the *isolation* of elements identified in earlier research and considered central to each approach to industrial relations management. But factor analysis is necessary to assess the extent of the relationship between items in each group and how far it is empirically justifiable to infer consultative and paternal 'styles' from these measures. This exercise revealed two (and only two) factors that directly corresponded with the two 'styles', accounted for 50.8 per cent of the shared variance, and clearly suggested that firms pursuing these distinctive 'styles' were satisfactorily isolated by the measures. The correlations between items in the consultative 'style' were highly significant ($p < 0.001$) and ranged from $r = 0.27$ to $r = 0.53$. For the paternal 'style', the first two items correlated at $r = 0.35$ ($p < 0.001$), though the relationships of these variables with the third item were not significant.

In table 5.3, the results are set out with the responses grouped according to the two 'styles' of industrial relations management. It will be seen that there is a clear relationship between each of the main independent variables and the existence or otherwise of all-employee schemes for profit sharing or share ownership. The effects are pronounced in the cases of companies where information sharing, employee involvement, and company loyalty are enhanced. However, the consultative decision-making 'style' is stronger than the paternal 'style' in predicting the presence of schemes (the two factors correlating with the dependent variable at $r = 0.26$ ($p < 0.001$) and $r = 0.16$ ($p < 0.005$) respectively). The correlations between the individual variables and each style are also shown in the table. It can be seen that in each case the correlation is substantially higher than the autocorrelation indicating a satisfactory level of internal consistency in the composite measure. This applies particularly to the consultative decision-making 'style' (where the correlations range from 0.71 to 0.77). These data reinforce the case that firms adopting this 'style' have been adequately located by the measures used in this research. They also underscore the view that this managerial approach to industrial relations (rather than paternalism) is the most central to the introduction of profit-sharing and share-ownership schemes.

Table 5.3 Company industrial relations policies and the presence of any all-employee scheme for profit sharing or share ownership

Scheme present = Yes Scheme absent = No	% who indicate policy very appropriate								% who indicate policy is not at all appropriate		Correlation with dependent variable	Correlation with composite variable
	1		2		3		4		5			
	Yes	No	Yes	No	Yes	No	Yes	No	Yes	No		
	%	%	%	%	%	%	%	%	%	%		
Consultative decision-making 'style':												
1 to *involve* employees in full partnership with management to serve the overall objectives of the company as a whole	25.1	10.7	28.6	22.3	28.0	30.1	12.6	23.3	5.7	13.6	0.25[a]	0.77
2 to *inform* employees or their representatives on a regular basis about company objectives and day-to-day management	39.1	17.4	30.5	33.9	21.3	26.6	6.9	13.8	2.3	8.3	0.25[a]	0.76

3 to accept that most employees are committed to their unions and hence to encourage collective bargaining on a regular basis	12.0	1.7	20.0	26.7	25.0	21.7	23.0	16.7	20.0	33.3	0.13[b]	0.71
Paternal decision-making 'style':												
4 to expect loyalty from employees in return for an advanced welfare package	26.8	18.3	39.6	23.1	27.4	34.6	4.3	14.7	1.8	9.6	0.27[a]	0.70
5 to encourage employees to fulfil their maximum potential	51.7	39.1	33.7	28.2	13.5	28.2	1.1	2.7	0	1.8	0.20[a]	0.61
6 to consider that the company's obligations to the workforce are confined only to working hours	1.8	7.5	15.4	15.1	29.0	30.2	20.7	23.6	33.1	23.6	-0.11[b]	0.56

Notes: Distribution on five-point item scales, correlations of items with the dependent variable, and with the composite scales of which they are a part assessing agreement with 'consultative' and 'paternal' decision-making 'styles' of industrial relations management.

$n = 303$; firms with schemes = 191; firms without schemes = 112; [a] significant at 0.001 level; [b] significant at 0.05 level. The correlations are based on scales omitting not applicable, don't know, and no answer scores. Positive correlations are with the (5) end of the scales.

None the less, although the relationship between managerial 'styles' in industrial relations and the adoption of schemes was found to be strong for the cases of companies with any generally based schemes and for those with SAYE-type arrangements, the association was very weak (and not statistically significant) for the APS variety. Based on the composite variables reflecting the consultative and paternal decision-making 'styles', table 5.4 thus sets out the relevant data. It will be noted that the variable assessing a consultative decision-making 'style' correlates with the adoption of any generally based schemes at $r = 0.26$ ($p < 0.001$) and with the SAYE schemes at $r = 0.24$ ($p < 0.001$). But there is only a very small and not significant link with the APS schemes ($r = 0.06$).

Table 5.4 Managerial industrial relations 'styles' and types of scheme for profit sharing and share ownership

	Any generally based scheme	Any scheme	APS	SAYE
Consultative decision-making 'style'	0.26[a]	0.20[b]	0.06	0.24[a]
Paternal decision-making 'style'	0.16[c]	0.12	0.10	0.13[c]

Notes: $n = 303$; Pearson product moment correlation coefficients; [a] significant at 0.001 level; [b]significant at 0.01 level; [c]significant at 0.05 level.
The consultative and paternal decision-making 'styles' are based on compositive variables derived from factor analysis. The variables in cash composite are set out in table 5.3.

Approved profit-sharing and SAYE schemes

In the case studies, managerial objectives in introducing schemes were explored in greater depth and it appeared that the APS schemes were seen particularly as inducements to employees to remain in a company. They act, as one company secretary noted, like a 'glue' – an incentive to continue to be a member of a specific firm. Hence it is scarcely surprising that firms embarking upon such schemes are particularly those which experience tight labour market conditions.

The SAYE schemes are far more linked with the broader objective of *employee involvement*. In phase 1 of the research, it was found that these schemes were clearly related to the industrial relations policies of companies on participation and employee involvement whereas APS schemes were rather different in this respect. The case studies revealed precisely why this situation obtains. For, whereas APS schemes are introduced by firms in tight labour market situations as a means of *attracting* and *retaining* employees, SAYE schemes are far more linked with strategies for employee involvement. And these can of course arise in firms with *varying* labour market situations. Moreover, as the survey revealed, it is scarcely surprising that firms introducing SAYE schemes are not only likely to have managements who base decisions on agreement with employees, but also other channels of employee involvement including staff associations and trade unions (see chapters 6 and 7).

To illustrate these points, it is worth listing a sample of some of the comments made about each of the main types of scheme from the case-study data.

Approved profit sharing
General manager: manufacturing company
   The main objective is that employees should benefit from the profits of the company. A secondary objective is to stimulate interest in company affairs.

Company secretary: finance company
   The main objective was to reward and keep the company's staff.

Company secretary: marketing company
   The objective is to give the staff a bonus in the form of shares ... it gives employees a stake in the company which is linked with profitability. It is a way of giving everybody in the company a stake in the company.

Save as you earn
Company secretary: manufacturing company
   To extend more employee participation and relate reward to company performance.

Company secretary: retail company
   To generate greater financial participation in the company. This fits in with the participatory methods of management in the company, which involves widespread consultation with the employees.

Personnel manager: finance company
   There is a genuine wish by the company to involve employees in understanding what the company does and the company feels that employees do have a better understanding of the company as a result of the schemes.

Nevertheless, it is important to note that nearly half of the case-study companies had both types of scheme and, sometimes, therefore, the various objectives were fused. Again, an illustrative sample of quotations is valuable here:

Director of finance: manufacturing company
There were three main objectives for the schemes: (1) to have the employees identify more with the overall objectives of the company in terms of its growth and profitability. Linked to this was the desire to improve commitment to middle and lower levels of the company; (2) to enable people to profit from the company's growth, in addition to their pay; and (3) it was felt that because of the way the schemes have been devised, a good employer should, as a matter of course, offer such schemes. This company considers itself to be a good employer and therefore is almost obliged to have schemes.

Company secretary: manufacturing company
An opportunity to participate in the capital growth of the company, to extend employee participation and to relate reward to company performance.

Company secretary: finance sector company
The reason for establishing some form of profit sharing/share ownership in the company was twofold. First, because it was believed that each employee has a right to a part of the company in which he/ she works. Secondly, because the management worked to increase each employee's stake in the company and hence increase their loyalty.

Notwithstanding the importance of economic infrastructure in accounting for the origins of schemes, it is clear from the foregoing analysis that the 'styles' of industrial relations adopted by managers in the firm are of considerable importance in understanding varying patterns of development of schemes in Britain as well. Indeed, it is precisely by means of an adequate understanding of the diverse motives and meanings of the initiators of the schemes that a comprehensive explanation for the emergence of the different forms of employee financial participation can be achieved.

Chapter six

Industrial relations climate

The different 'styles' adopted by management in the sphere of employee relations are to be expected to be interlinked with the broader climate of industrial relations in the firm as a whole. As has been noted in the theoretical analysis in chapter 2, there are strong grounds for assuming that managements have increasingly sought to foster a wide range of employee-participation practices designed to enhance commitment to the company. Moreover, it is also probable that firms with an advanced participatory climate (reflected in the institutionalization of various procedures for employee involvement) will be the most likely to have adopted schemes for employee financial participation.

In this chapter, these issues are assessed in depth and detail by examining the extent to which firms in which managements regularly reach decisions after a process of consultation and agreement (and in which several types of machinery for employee involvement have been installed) are also likely to have programmes for profit sharing and share ownership. Survey data are reinforced by case-study material to reveal the extent to which employee financial participation stems from an overall employee-involvement policy in the firm. The industrial relations climate of the enterprise is then shown to be more strongly related to the adoption of schemes than the existence of incentive and other variable payment systems.

Employee participation in decision making

The argument from industrial relations 'climate' rests on two central propositions. The first is that it is reasonable to regard the various forms of organizational democracy (economic and industrial) as intertwined, so long as the types under consideration are reasonably cognate. To be sure, this relationship will not always obtain, but it is probable that an overall employee-involvement policy in the company will occasion changes in the financial status of employees and in their opportunities to participate in decision making. And the second is that the 'favourable conjunctures' underpinning the advance of both forms of workplace democracy are more consistent with an evolutionary rather than a cyclical interpretation of long-term trends in the growth of organizational democracy itself.

To assess these arguments in detail, based on the work of Gallie (1978), respondents in the 'main-stage' survey were asked to what extent a series of decisions were typically taken by management alone, after consultation, or after agreement/negotiation. The issues covered wages and salaries, safety and health, discipline, the introduction of new technology, shift and overtime working, manning levels, an increase or reduction in the workforce, investment in new units, and the allocation of profits to wages or investment. The results are presented in table 6.1 where it will be seen that there is a clear tendency for firms in which management shares decision making to be likely to have one or more of the various all-employee profit-sharing or shareholding schemes. The relationship is particularly marked in companies where there is joint decision making on manning levels, the introduction of new technology, and an increase or reduction in the workforce. However, although employee participation in industrial relations decisions is connected with the adoption of profit-sharing and share-ownership schemes, this linkage does not apply to involvement in financial-type issues.

The responses on the industrial relations variables were all highly intercorrelated ($p < 0.001$) ranging from $r = 0.41$ to $r = 0.62$ and the scores were added to give a composite measure. The correlations between items and the overall scores are shown in the table. As may be seen, the correlations are typically high and, even allowing for the autocorrelation effect, indicate a satisfactory level of internal consistency. Moreover, there is a fairly strong relationship between the overall factor indicating employee participation in industrial relations issues and the presence of schemes in the company ($r = 0.23$, $p < 0.001$).

It should be emphasized, however, that this broad pattern of relationship does not apply for all the types of profit sharing and share ownership. Indeed, for reasons already given, APS schemes appear to be developed largely independently of the industrial relations patterns of the company as a whole. Hence, as is shown in table 6.2, there are appreciable differences between the degree of relationship between decision-making patterns in firms and the adoption of SAYE and APS schemes respectively. Furthermore,

Table 6.1 Patterns of decision making in companies and the presence of any all-employee scheme for profit sharing or share ownership

Decisions taken by: Scheme present = Yes Scheme absent = No	Management alone 1		After consultation 2		After negotiation/ agreement 3		Correlation with dependent variable	Correlation with composite variable
	Yes	No	Yes	No	Yes	No		
	%	%	%	%	%	%		
Industrial relations issues:								
1 wages and salaries	47.7	51.8	10.2	13.6	42.0	34.5	0.06	0.79
2 safety and health	31.8	44.8	41.0	37.4	27.2	17.8	0.14[b]	0.76
3 discipline	65.1	68.5	17.1	20.4	17.7	11.1	0.07	0.72
4 introduction of new technology	52.3	65.2	27.1	26.1	20.6	8.7	0.16[b]	0.73
5 shift or overtime working	38.0	51.7	30.7	25.8	31.3	22.5	0.13[c]	0.78
6 manning levels	57.0	77.3	21.8	15.5	21.2	7.2	0.22[a]	0.78
7 increase/decrease of the workforce	58.5	74.1	22.2	14.8	19.3	11.1	0.15[b]	0.72
Financial issues:								
8 investment in new units	93.1	95.2	6.4	2.9	0.6	1.9	0.01	0.84
9 allocations of profits into wages/investment	96.4	100.0	2.4	0	1.2	0	0.01	0.61

Notes: Distribution on three-point scales, correlations with dependent variable, and with the composite scales of which they are a part assessing employee involvement in industrial relations and financial issues.

n = 303; firms with schemes = 191; firms without schemes = 112; [a] significant at 0.001 level; [b] significant at 0.01 level; [c] significant at 0.05 level. The correlations are based on scales omitting not applicable, don't know, and no answer scores. Positive correlations are with the (3) end of the scale.

while there are highly significant correlations between industrial relations decision-making practices and the adoption of SAYE schemes in firms, these relationships do not apply in the case of the APS schemes.

Respondents were also asked whether a number of channels for employee participation existed in their companies. These included joint consultation, productivity bargaining, new technology agreements, formal collective bargaining, informal collective bargaining, regular meetings between supervisors and workgroups, job redesign, quality circles, and management committees with employee or union representation. The results are set out in table 6.3 where it will be noted that there is a consistent tendency for companies with any of the main variations of all-employee profit-sharing or share-ownership schemes to be the most likely to have these various types of employee participation. The particularly significant relationship with the existence of joint consultative machinery reinforces the findings presented in chapter 5 on the importance of a consultative 'style' of industrial relations management for the development of all-employee schemes for profit sharing and share ownership.

The answers were factor analysed, a procedure which revealed two clusters of types of employee participation. The main items loading on each of these factors were added together to provide composite scores covering largely trade union and non-trade union participation bodies respectively (the range of consistently significant ($p < 0.001$) correlations amongst items in the first factor being $r = 0.22$ to $r = 0.57$ and in the second $r = 0.24$ and $r = 0.34$). The correlations between the items forming part of each scale and the composite scores are also shown in table 6.3. In each case they are noticeably higher than the autocorrelation effect alone, indicating an acceptable level of internal consistency. In addition, both factors correlate with the dependent variable at $r = 0.21$ ($p < 0.001$) reinforcing the clear patterning of data which indicate a link between the adoption of profit-sharing and share-ownership schemes and a consultative decision-making 'style' of industrial relations.

But once again it is important to disaggregate the dependent variable because different patterns apply for APS and SAYE schemes respectively. In table 6.4 the relevant correlational data are presented and it will be readily apparent that the highly significant relationships between the presence of various employee participation channels and the adoption of SAYE schemes do not obtain for the APS variety.

Table 6.2 Decision making in companies and profit sharing or share ownership (Pearson product moment correlation coefficients) (extent to which decisions on selected issues are taken by (1) management alone, (2) after consultation, or (3) by negotiation/agreement)

Decision areas	Any scheme	Inland Revenue-approved profit-sharing (APS) scheme	Inland Revenue-approved save as you earn (SAYE) scheme	Factor loading
Factor 1 Industrial relations issues:				
1 wages and salaries	0.09	−0.05	0.21[a]	0.78
2 safety and health	0.16[b]	−0.05	0.22[a]	0.77
3 discipline	0.10	−0.05	0.13[c]	0.71
4 introduction of new technology	0.15[b]	0.04	0.28[a]	0.70
5 shift or overtime	0.20[a]	0.02	0.22[a]	0.81
6 manning levels	0.20[a]	0.06	0.19[a]	0.68
7 increase/decrease of the workforce	0.17[b]	0.06	0.19[a]	0.68
Factor 2 Financial issues:				
8 investment in new units	−0.01	−0.02	0.01	0.65
9 allocation of profits	0.09	−0.04	0.07	0.79

Notes: The numbers range between 239 and 286: [a]significant at 0.001 level; [b]significant at 0.01 level; [c]significant at 0.05 level. The two factors account for 57.8 per cent of the shared variance. Positive correlations are with the (3) end of the scale.

Table 6.3 Patterns of employee participation and the existence of any all-employee schemes for profit sharing or share ownership: percentage distributions, correlations with dependent variable, and with composite variables indicating union- and non-union-based participation bodies

	Presence of any all-employee scheme	No all-employee scheme	Correlation with dependent variable	Correlation with composite variable
	%	%		
Typically union-based participation bodies:				
1 joint consultation/works council meetings	53	29	0.23[a]	0.76
2 productivity bargaining	32	21	0.12[c]	0.78
3 new technology agreements	24	13	0.13[c]	0.66
4 formal collective bargaining	45	29	0.16[b]	0.80
5 informal collective bargaining	28	18	0.12[c]	0.82
Typically non-union-based participation bodies:				
1 regular meetings between supervisors and workgroups	68	49	0.18[a]	0.74
2 job redesign involving employees or their representatives	27	19	0.10	0.70
3 quality circles	26	14	0.13[b]	0.68
4 management committees where there is employee or union representation	36	20	0.17[b]	0.66

Notes: n = 303; [a] significant at 0.001 level; [b] significant at 0.01 level; [c] significant at 0.05 level. The correlations are based on scores from yes/no answers.

Table 6.4 Employee participation and profit sharing or share ownership (Pearson product moment correlation coefficients)

Types of participation	Any scheme	Inland Revenue-approved profit-sharing (APS) scheme	Inland Revenue-approved save as you earn (SAVE) scheme	Factor loading
Factor 1 Typically union-based participation bodies:				
1 joint consultation/works council meetings	0.21[a]	0.04	0.20[a]	0.59
2 productivity bargaining	0.15[b]	−0.06	0.17[a]	0.77
3 new technology agreements	0.13[b]	−0.05	0.24[a]	0.48
4 formal collective bargaining	0.15[b]	0.02	0.28[a]	0.78
5 informal collective bargaining	0.12[c]	−0.07	0.14[b]	0.69
Factor 2 Typically non-union-based participation bodies:				
1 regular meetings between supervisors and workgroups	0.24[a]	0.02	0.20[a]	0.61
2 job redesign involving employees or their representatives	0.08	−0.03	0.18[a]	0.73
3 quality circles	0.16[b]	−0.09	0.10[c]	0.70
4 management committees where there is employee or union representation	0.15[b]	0.01	0.11[c]	0.61

Notes: $n = 303$; [a] significant at 0.001 level; [b] significant at 0.01 level; [c] significant at 0.05 level. The two factors account for 52.1 per cent of the shared variance.

Indeed, using factors, the composite variables indicating the presence of union-based and non-union-based participation bodies in the company correlate with the presence of SAYE schemes at $r = 0.28$ ($p < 0.001$) and $r = 0.21$ ($p < 0.001$) respectively. For the APS schemes the relevant correlations were both $r = 0.03$ and were not statistically significant. Hence, while there is general support for the industrial relations climate thesis, it is necessary to qualify the argument to exclude APS schemes.

Case-study data

Turning to the case-study data, a clear finding was that, amongst firms with early schemes in particular, the development of profit sharing and share ownership is linked with industrial relations policies on employee involvement. To be sure, these policies do not emerge in an entirely voluntary manner. Indeed, they almost certainly stem not only from managerial preferences for particular approaches but also from external labour market conditions, company structure (and particularly size of organization), and the patterns of trade unionism and other aspects of industrial relations within a given firm.

But there is a connection between industrial relations policy and employee financial participation that appears to be particularly evident in the manufacturing sector and in firms with trade unions. There are four main manifestations here: (1) the link with so-called 'codetermination'; (2) policy on involvement of trade unions; (3) a coherent company management philosophy of which indus-trial relations is a part; and (4) the relevance of employee financial participation to a changing industrial relations climate. The first case (1) is illustrated by information obtained in a leading manu-facturing concern:

> The company has a long history of co-determination through collective bargaining and joint consultation and evaluation for two main groups – staff and hourly-paid. There exists an extensive structure of consultative/productivity committees throughout the company at all levels. Share-ownership schemes are seen as an extension of this participation arrangement.

The case of a unionized retailing firm indicates the second point (2):

> It is the policy of the company that trade union membership is a matter for personal decision and it is clearly understood that staff have a legal right to belong, or not to belong, to any trade

union. The company believes that fully representative unions have a useful part to play in achieving the successful, economic and profitable running of the business and welcomes full communication and consultation on all matters affecting employment. It is important that as many staff as possible belong to any union which has been officially recognised by the company to represent their interests so that agreements reached between the company and the union have the commitment of the greater majority of staff. It is agreed policy that, wherever possible, routine matters will be dealt with directly between management and staff at department level. The schemes were discussed with unions prior to introducing them.

The link with an overall management philosophy, revealed in the case of a unionized manufacturing company, illustrated not only the connection between employee involvement and profit sharing and share ownership, but also the way in which management assessed the impact of schemes (3).

The overall industrial relations policy is seen in terms of developing a company culture or management style. This identifies rules of behaviour for management throughout the company. Financial participation is a long term policy for the company, therefore, whether it directly improves efficiency is largely an 'act of faith'.

The fourth instance (4) emerged in another manufacturing concern.

The company has several aims: to be a good employer, to pay highly, to communicate with staff and to offer good career prospects. The company aims to be very consultative. Whereas previously the company operated under what was termed a more bureaucratic egalitarian basis, it is now moving towards a more individualistic approach, which attempts to motivate appropriate people in appropriate ways. The schemes are a reflection of this, and together they give a unity of purpose.

In short, in this particular company, the earliest types of collective agreements were being slowly changed, together with the 'bureaucratic' approach which this reflected. This was being transformed to a more individually focused and consultative-type approach in which profit sharing and share ownership for employees was a signal feature.

Key representatives were asked whether, following the intro-duction of profit-sharing or share-ownership schemes, changes occurred in *other* modes of employee involvement. In the vast majority of firms, it was argued that there had been no discernible reciprocal effect of schemes on employee-involvement policy.

Indeed, the overwhelming response was that any reciprocal relationship was largely *indirect* and, as the company secretary of a manufacturing concern argued, 'company employee involvement policy was responsible for introducing the schemes rather than the other way around'. In short, the overall climate of industrial relations is highly relevant to the introduction of most all-employee schemes for profit sharing and share ownership. This is further enhanced by the presence of schemes, but these are not generally the spur for wider changes in employee-involvement practices themselves.

Pay policy and payment systems

Part of the case for extending employee financial participation has always rested upon its potential as a flexible system of remuneration and reward that is attuned to wider market forces. Hence, the study would not be complete without some reference to the relationship between flexible payment systems and the origins and development of profit-sharing and share-ownership schemes.

Although, as we have seen, there is an association between participatory practices and general forms of profit sharing and employee shareholding, it is of course conceivable that the main stimulus for companies to introduce such schemes arises from an advanced strategy for motivating and rewarding employees linked with an overarching pay policy and incentive payment system. After all, in recent years, incentive packages within enterprise have undoubtedly become highly sophisticated. To assess the effects of pay policy and incentive payment systems in the 'main-stage' survey, respondents were asked to what extent company policy was to pay above the average for a particular industry or service. Further information was also elicited on the existence of other incentive payment systems (notably payment by results, individual and plant-wide bonus schemes, commission, or other incentive *systems*). These items were found to form *a single-payment systems factor* that accounted for 34.1 per cent of the variance.

The overall results are set out in table 6.5 where it will be seen that there is a very weak link between pay policy and the adoption of profit sharing or share ownership, a relationship that is explained by the modest but significant correlation with APS schemes. But there are very few connections between most types of

Table 6.5 Pay policy, incentive payment systems, and profit sharing or share ownership (Pearson product moment correlation coefficients)

	General scheme	Any scheme	Inland Revenue-approved profit-sharing (APS) scheme	Inland Revenue-approved save as you earn (SAYE) scheme	Factor loading
Pay policy[d]					
Pay above average (five-point scale) (n = 278)	0.14[b]	0.09	0.16[b]	-0.05	
Payment systems (one factor) (n = 303)					
Payment by results	0.01	0.00	-0.11	0.03	0.68
Individual bonus	-0.01	0.02	-0.09	0.13[a]	0.61
Plant-wide bonus	0.13[b]	0.13[c]	-0.09	0.20[a]	0.49
Commission	0.08	0.09	0.01	0.10[c]	0.64
Other	0.02	-0.01	0.10	-0.04	-0.47

Notes: n = 303; none of the correlation coefficients is significant at [a] 0.001 level in the first three columns; [b] significant at 0.01 level; [c] significant at 0.05 level. [d] Positive correlations are with the (5) point of the scale. Factor analysis yielded a single factor which accounted for 34.1 per cent of the variance.

payment systems and the existence of any of the all-employee schemes for profit sharing or share ownership (the only partial exception being for the existence of plant-wide bonuses in the firm). The SAYE schemes are slightly but not appreciably different from the general pattern, but it does seem clear that profit-sharing and share-ownership schemes do not stem in any obvious way from modern incentive and reward packages within companies. Rather a number of characteristics of the enterprises themselves, managerial 'styles', and the industrial relations climate of the firm reflected in employee-participation practices are far more important influences.

Chapter seven

Collective representation

But the development of employee financial participation also rests upon the policies of employee collectivities (and notably trade unions and staff associations). As was noted in chapter 1, classical theorists of the labour movement viewed the growth of profit sharing with considerable circumspection. Indeed, over seventy years ago, in a special supplement to the *New Statesman*, the Webbs (1914: 24) not only argued that 'on the ordinary principles of prudence . . . the very last investment that a workman ought to choose for his savings is the industry – least of all the very enterprise – on which he depends for his daily bread', but also observed a number of potentially deleterious consequences for trade unions:

> as a matter of experience profit-sharing schemes are distinctly adverse to Trade Union membership, even where there is no express prohibition of it . . . [Trade Unionists] regard the whole basis of the sharing of profits as unfair. It is always argued by the advocates of profit sharing, and always expected by employers, that the employees will, by their increased energy, zeal, docility, regularity and avoidance of waste, themselves produce the increased profit. It does not seem to them fair that they should be graciously awarded, as a favour, a share only of the new surplus that they have produced.

It is vital at this point, then, to establish in detail the current attitudes of trade unionists on profit sharing and share ownership. The relationship between trade unions and staff associations and the development of employee financial participation in the firm is first assessed. This is followed by: (1) an analysis of case-study data on the views of active trade unionists; (2) an examination of the interrelationships between the main industrial relations variables; and (3) a discussion of the effects of size of enterprise on trade unions and other related phenomena.

Survey data

In order to assess the relationship (if any) between trade unionism and profit sharing and share ownership, respondents in the survey stage of the research were asked whether or not there was a trade union or staff association in their enterprises, while supplementary material was also gathered on the density of unionism (i.e. the proportion of the workforce in trade unions) and on the presence of a manual closed shop. In table 7.1, the main results are set out and it will be seen that there is an association between the adoption by firms of a generally based or any scheme for profit sharing and share ownership and the existence of trade unions and staff associations. However, the presence of staff associations rather than trade unions is shown to be the better predictor of the adoption of schemes ($\phi = 0.51$, $p < 0.0001$ compared with $\phi = 0.18$, $p < 0.002$).

Indeed, if the standardizing effect of the size of the firm (measured by capital assets) is included, the relationship between trade union presence and all-employee profit-sharing and share-ownership schemes largely disappears (the relationship between trade union presence and capital assets of the firm is $r = 0.21$; $p < 0.001$). However, although the link between the presence of staff associations and capital assets of the firm is $r = 0.33$ ($p < 0.001$), of all the explanatory and standardizing variables examined, the existence of staff associations is the strongest single predictor of the presence of all-employee schemes for profit sharing and share ownership.

This pattern may stem partly from the fact that, while both consultative and paternal 'styles' of industrial relations management are conducive to the growth of staff associations, only the former are typically consistent with flourishing trade unionism. Hence, it was found that while a consultative 'style' correlates with the presence of trade unions and staff associations at the $p < 0.01$ level ($r = 0.21$ and $r = 0.22$ respectively), there is no relationship between a paternal 'style' and the existence of trade unions, even though the correlation with staff associations remains significant ($r = 0.15$, $p < 0.01$). It is also worth mentioning that although density of unionism in the firm is significantly but not strongly linked with the presence of all-employee schemes for profit sharing and share ownership, there is no further effect of the existence of a manual closed shop.

Nevertheless, there are pronounced differences in the effects of trade unionism depending on the types of scheme. This is clearly demonstrated by the use of correlational data. Table 7.2 thus

Table 7.1 Collective representation and profit sharing or share ownership (n = 302)

Trade union/ staff association membership	General scheme		Any scheme		Inland Revenue-approved profit-sharing (APS) scheme		Inland Revenue-approved save as you earn (SAYE) scheme	
	Yes	No	Yes	No	Yes	No	Yes	No
Trade union (TU)	140	63	159	44	42	161	101	102
Staff association (SA)	128	16	132	12	42	102	100	44
Neither	49	47	60	36	26	70	17	79
Density of unionism (n = 257–301)								
None	51	49	62	38	27	73	49	95
1 – 24%	36	14	41	9	15	35	18	32
25 – 49%	16	13	20	9	4	25	12	17
50 – 74%	31	13	36	8	6	38	24	20
75 – 90%	23	11	26	8	8	26	17	17
Manual closed shop (n = 201)								
Full	19	9	20	8	7	21	13	15
Partial	27	10	32	5	7	30	25	12
None	91	45	104	32	30	106	56	80

Notes: For general scheme: TU or SA present: chi-square = 7.8 (degrees of freedom = 1), significance = 0.005, ϕ = 0.17; density of unionism: chi-square = 9.5 (degrees of freedom = 4), significance = 0.05, Cramer's V = 0.19; manual closed shop: not significant. For any scheme: TU or SA present: chi-square = 6.9 (degrees of freedom = 1), significance = 0.009, ϕ = 0.16; density of unionism: chi-square = 6.9 (degrees of freedom = 1), significance = 0.04, Cramer's V = 0.20; manual closed shop: not significant. For Inland Revenue-approved profit-sharing (APS) scheme: none of the relationships is significant. For Inland Revenue-approved save as you earn (SAYE) scheme: TU or SA present: chi-square = 26.43 (degrees of freedom = 1), significance = 0.0001, ϕ = 0.30; density of unionism: not significant; closed shop: chi-square = 8.1 (degrees of freedom = 2), significance = 0.02, Cramer's V = 0.20.

reveals the strong links between the adoption of SAYE schemes and the presence of staff associations ($r = 0.59$), trade unions ($r = 0.30$), and trade union density ($r = 0.28$).

For the APS schemes, however, although the presence of staff associations is a weak predictor of their presence in the firm ($r = 0.15, p < 0.01$), their relationship with the trade union variables is not statistically significant.

Table 7.2 Collective representation in the firm and the various types of employee financial participation ($n = 303$) (Pearson product moment correlation coefficients)

	Any generally based (i.e. all-employee) scheme	Any scheme	APS	SAYE
Collective representation:				
presence of staff association in enterprises	0.51[a]	0.40[a]	0.15[b]	0.59[a]
presence of union in enterprises	0.18[a]	0.18[a]	-0.06	0.30[a]
higher rather than lower degree of unionism	0.12	0.11	-0.10	0.28[a]
manual closed shop	-0.02	0.00	-0.06	-0.10

Note: [a]significant at 0.001 level; [b]significant at 0.01 level.

Case-study data

Turning to the case-study data, the views of trade union activists (shop stewards and full-time officials) on profit sharing and share ownership were found to be largely of lukewarm or passive acceptance. However, there was little enthusiasm for linking pay with profits in a way which affected traditional collective bargaining and a minority of union officials opposed profit sharing. Typically, union officials felt their members would prefer a cash bonus or a general pay rise to profit sharing through share schemes. However, so long as the schemes were kept away from conventional bargaining channels, there was little widespread opposition.

Indeed, a number of interviews were carried out with both full-time union officials and shop stewards (and other union representatives) at establishment level (see the preface for details). The principal findings discussed below are: (1) the lack of coherent union and inter-union policies on profit sharing and share ownership; (2) qualified approval for APS and SAYE schemes; (3) the preference for flat-rate allocations; and (4) some opposition to ESO schemes.

Trade union representatives were asked first of all whether or not there was a general union policy on profit sharing and share ownership. A typical response was from an Amalgamated Engineering Union (AEU) shop steward who indicated that there was 'no typical line or policy on profit sharing/share ownership other than the decision to take shares in the company should be left to the individual member and that negotiations about pay should be kept separate from share schemes'. A more detailed view was put forward by a chairman of the staff unions in a manufacturing concern:

> The union is in favour of profit-sharing schemes so long as they do not prejudice pay negotiations. There is, however, some disquiet that income from share schemes is not pensionable. Also, share schemes are at the total discretion of management when they should be more directly related to profits, i.e. an automatic percentage payment. Management are trying to keep basic pay rises down to a minimum with the carrot of shares. The company has been continually trying to introduce profit sharing into pay negotiations while the union has been trying to develop, for a number of years, a bonus scheme linked to profits.
>
> There is some prejudice in the union against company handouts of shares. Also, the shares should be free and the distribution of shares should be across the board not based on grade, length of service, etc. The latter may mean that the schemes are 'divisive'. A flat rate handout would be the fairest system since it is the lower grades who produce the products and it is to them that the shares should be directed.

Moreover, although at establishment level, unions did attempt to formulate consistent inter-union positions in specific cases (e.g. when management endeavoured to link pay and profit sharing), in general no coherent overall position appeared to have emerged at this level. This was also evident in our discussions with full-time officials outside the plant. The full-time officers we interviewed did not generally oppose profit sharing or share ownership but it was not an issue to which they attached significance, unless it led to complications for the collective bargaining process.

Moreover, when union representatives were asked about their views on specific schemes, it was clear that there was *broad* support for the APS and SAYE types. In general, there was a preference for 'flat-rate' modes of allocation and it was widely felt that these schemes had no motivational effect whatsoever for lower grades. As one representative noted with respect to a SAYE scheme:

> Financial commitment to the scheme depends on financial circumstances which largely depends on an employee's position in the company. It is considered as a scheme for higher grades. Not motivational to the extent that management would like. Motivation of the lower grades is neglected by the scheme.

And as a union colleague in the same firm argued:

> The scheme can be good if worked properly. However, share prices are too high now for those in the lower wage bracket. This means that individuals who cannot afford to take up share options or save more lose out. The schemes are not really designed for those on the lower wage brackets; they are more of a gamble, particularly if the share price is high. Also, they are influenced by the price of the dollar because of the large amount of products the company exports.

But with the ESO types of scheme there was far more noticeable union hostility. This view of another AEU official was not untypical:

> ESOs smack of nepotism and there is a lot of disquiet amongst the staff. Senior executives have been given 'pots of gold' – no savings, no commitment at all. Management could also be accused of double standards by continually emphasising in pay rounds that employees 'should tighten their belts' and then they offer this scheme to management. The argument given is that this prevents experienced senior executives from leaving the company yet turnover amongst these grades is insignificant.

And the chairman of a union section which covered two sites in a major manufacturing company noted some negative consequences of ESO schemes for attitudes in negotiations:

> The union does not approve of this type of scheme. It is a way of distorting a negotiated settlement and perceived as such by the staff. A way of senior management to profit themselves not available to other staff. This will lead to a higher level of 'emotion' in pay negotiations enhancing the element of 'us' and 'them' and is thus potentially divisive. Its one advantage is that it may be of help to recruit more able senior management – though there is no evidence of that in the company. It is therefore seen by employees as 'manipulative and counter-productive'. There has been no attempt to justify ESOs by management.

But on the basis of the case studies, it is clear that the relationship between collective representation and employee financial participation stems more from management than trade union policies. We have seen that trade union views on profit sharing and share ownership are ambivalent and tend to be lukewarm rather than either enthusiastically supportive or implacably hostile. By contrast, managements which are prepared to recognize trade unions, to consult and to negotiate with them, and to involve representatives on formal and informal committees are undoubtedly those which are in turn favourable to *other* modes of employee involvement including financial participation.

The following statements help to reveal further aspects of the pattern:

Manufacturing company (70 per cent unionization)
The first three unions act together and tend to be more like staff associations. There is one collective bargaining agreement with the first three, and individual ones with each of the others. The company consults on a wide basis. The company does try to keep the schemes out of negotiations, though each of the above unions was widely consulted prior to the introduction of schemes.

Manufacturing company (85 per cent unionization)
Informal meetings were held with trade union representatives before the introduction of the schemes. Concern was expressed about the loss of the cash bonus scheme but the unions welcomed the employee share schemes as an extension of industrial democracy albeit at the margin. Consultation about the schemes continues.

Finance sector company (65 per cent unionization)
Consultative briefings operate throughout all levels of the company. Negotiations are centralised. Schemes are non-negotiable and seen as totally separate from the negotiations, though consultation takes place over the schemes. This arrangement is partly because of legislative involvement in the operation of the schemes for this cannot be negotiated.

Finance sector company (50 per cent unionization)
The union management procedural agreement makes very little contribution to profit sharing and share ownership schemes in the company. There is a centralised negotiating and consultative system under the procedural agreement. Profit sharing schemes are an issue which is raised at the central consultative meetings e.g. the interpretation of rules have been agreed with the unions.

Manufacturing company (50–55 per cent unionization)
Procedural agreements are negotiated in between 40–50 local units organised by geographical area and business sector. All bargaining units are largely independent from central control. Only share schemes and pensions are nationally organised. There was no consultation with trade unions over the introduction of the schemes. Schemes are not seen as bargaining ploy/tactic. They are sometimes discussed at consultative committees but this is only to improve understanding.

In short, there is little *direct* relationship between trade union participation and profit sharing and share ownership. The positive relationship between trade unionism and employee financial participation discovered in the survey stage thus stems from the broad tendency for firms with collective bargaining also to be those in which other ideas for extending employee involvement, such as share ownership schemes, are encouraged.

Industrial relations and size of organization

It is clear then that there are a number of interconnected elements of the industrial relations policies and practices in companies in Britain that are associated with the varied adoption of schemes for employee financial participation. As we have seen from the survey data, these include a consultative 'style' of industrial relations management, the extent to which decisions on industrial relations are based on agreement, the existence of typically union- and non-union-based bodies for employee participation, and the presence of trade unions and staff associations. The strong interrelationships between these variables are shown in table 7.3 (indeed, it will be noted that all the correlations are significant at least at the $p < 0.01$ level). These data thus clearly point to a pronounced patterning of industrial relations in firms in Britain that is highly relevant to understanding the uneven advance of profit-sharing and share-ownership schemes.

Given the importance of size of capital assets amongst the enterprise variables and its effects upon trade unionism in the firm, a further analysis of the links with the other independent variables is instructive at this point. The relevant data from the main-stage survey are set out in table 7.4 and suggest the following inferences. First, there is not a very consistent pattern of association amongst the economic 'infrastructure' variables. The size of capital assets of the firm is linked with annual turnover, the enterprise being in the financial sector and having a multi- rather than single-establishment

Table 7.3 Correlation coefficients between variables associated with company industrial relations policies and other main independent variables

	Pearson product moment coefficients					
	1	2	3	4	5	6
1 Consultative decision-making 'style'	–					
2 Extent to which decision making on industrial relations issues is based on agreement	0.43[a]	–				
3 Presence of union-type participation bodies	0.27[a]	0.61[a]	–			
4 Presence of non-union-type participation bodies	0.35[a]	0.40[a]	0.58[a]	–		
5 Presence of trade unions	0.21[b]	0.50[a]	0.56[a]	0.34[a]	–	
6 Presence of staff associations	0.22[b]	0.46[b]	0.47[a]	0.27[a]	0.62[a]	–

Notes: The numbers range between 157 and 302: [a]significant at 0.001 level; [b]significant at 0.01 level. The presence of union-type and non-union-type participative bodies are composite variables based on factor analysis (the full list of variables in each factor is shown in table 6.4). Variables 1 and 2 are also composites, the variables in each composite being set out in tables 5.3 and 6.1 respectively.

structure. But establishment autonomy and trends in the workforce and in business volume are not related to company size. Second, the management industrial relations 'styles' clearly occur independently of the capital assets of the firm and suggest a considerable measure of *choice* in the selection of various approaches to labour issues. There are, however, links between organizational size and the main forms of employee participation and collective representation, although these are generally not as strong or consistent as that obtaining for the cluster of industrial relations variables analysed and set out in table 7.3. Hence, even though the industrial relations climate of the firm is linked in part to the size of the employing enterprise, the inconsistent pattern of effects suggests a substantial measure of choice within companies in the types of management–employee relationships which emerge. Moreover, these findings underscore the general theoretical case established in this volume that the motives and meanings of the key personnel in the organization have to be understood if a satisfactory explanation for the diverse patterns of adoption of schemes for profit sharing and share ownership is to emerge.

Table 7.4 Capital assets of enterprises and groups of explanatory variables

	Pearson product moment correlation coefficients
Enterprise characteristics:	
enterprise in financial sector	0.30[a]
multi- rather than single establishment	0.26[a]
higher rather than lower extent of autonomy	−0.08
extent of increase in workforce	0.05
extent of increase in business volume	−0.18[b]
higher rather than lower annual turnover	0.69[a]
Management decision making[c]:	
consultative decision-making 'style'	0.13
paternal decision-making 'style'	0.10
Employee participation[d]:	
extent to which decision making on industrial relations issues based on agreement	0.19[b]
extent to which decision making on financial issues based on agreement	0.09
presence of union-based participation bodies	0.23[a]
presence of non-union-based participation bodies	0.24[a]
Payment systems[e]:	
policy to pay above average	0.13[b]
presence of other incentive payment systems	0.07
Collective representation:	
presence of staff association in enterprise	0.34[a]
presence of union in enterprise	0.21[a]
higher rather than lower degree of unionism	0.18[b]
manual closed shop	−0.00

Notes: The numbers range between 178 and 265: [a] significant at 0.001 level; [b] significant at 0.01 level.
[c] Based on composite variables from factor analysis; the full list of variables is set out in table 5.3.
[d] Details of the variables are set out in tables 6.1 and 6.2.
[e] Details of the variables are set out in table 6.5.

Chapter eight

Conclusions

In this first of two volumes on the subject, the aim has been to interpret and to explain the origins and development of profit-sharing and employee-shareholding schemes with special reference to the British experience. The bulk of the material which has been reported has stemmed from the survey and case-study phases of a project sponsored by the Department of Employment. It is hoped that the objectives of the study have, for the most part, been fulfilled and that an extensive range of material has been presented on a concern vital to management–employee relations as a whole. It remains to restate those arguments to which a special significance is attached and to elicit a number of salient conclusions from the findings of the study as a whole.

There has been a long-standing interest in profit sharing and other forms of employee financial participation. Advocates of these schemes have not infrequently viewed them as integral to a property-owning democracy. Moreover, under such social arrangements, it has been claimed that conflict between capital and labour would be eradicated by industrial partnership and that philosophies aimed at eliminating the system of private capitalism would become a spent force. However, on another view (expressed by classical theorists of the labour movement), profit sharing is inconsistent with trade union organization and action because it undermines the basic 'community of interests' which are integral to effective collective bargaining.

As it happens, our conclusions are that neither of these sharply contrasting ideological positions appear to have substantially impacted upon the advance of profit sharing. The early periods of development were thus almost invariably accompanied by a *growth* in trade union activity. Moreover, although during the 1980s expansion, trade unionism in the UK has declined, it is doubtful whether profit sharing has been at all responsible. And, in any event, the facilitative legislation which has accelerated the spread of employee financial participation has diverse ideological underpinnings which are only in part related to the notion of a property-owning democracy itself. Furthermore, the international experience of profit sharing reveals the coexistence of a substantial *variety* of institutionalized practices which are not obviously associated with trade unionism. In some countries, such as the USA and Sweden, there has been an appreciable expansion of schemes. But in other nations, such as West Germany, despite the fact that industrial democracy is a durable characteristic of management–employee relations, until very recently there has been no commensurate expansion of profit sharing and employee shareholding.

To explain the origins and development of employee financial participation is thus a difficult and controversial undertaking. Ideally, it requires the analyst to specify: (1) an *overall theory* of organizational democracy in which its main elements (economic and industrial) are integrated; (2) a *temporal theory* based on the notion of 'favourable conjunctures' that is not exclusively wedded to either an evolutionary or cyclical interpretation of long-term trends; (3) a *comparative theory* in which diverse governmental and legislative supports are accorded a central position; and (4) a *spatial theory* in which there is acknowledgement of both economic 'infrastructural' conditions and the varied motives, meanings, and power of the industrial relations 'actors'.

The general theory of organizational democracy is thus based on a synthesis of the notions of economic and industrial democracy. Economic democracy covers a variety of forms of employee financial participation in the ownership of enterprises and in the distribution of economic rewards. By contrast, industrial democracy encapsulates the notion of worker participation in decision making and employee involvement in the processes of control within the firm. These practices are, to some extent, coterminous, but they by no means invariably advance in parallel.

The thesis of 'favourable conjunctures' is basic to the elaboration of an overall inclusive theory. It encapsulates the notion of an uneven but advancing pattern which depends greatly on the different *circumstances* and *situations* which obtain between and within particular nations. To interpret long-term movements, this approach is to be preferred to the earlier evolutionary position in which a smooth 'onward and outward' progression has been depicted, and to the cyclical position which is too rhythmic in its implicit assumptions, unsatisfactory as a comparative theory, and unable to account for the very broad overall process of *uneven advance* which is evident.

Of course it could be argued that the ubiquity of the notion of 'favourable conjunctures' is a vulnerable point of the theory because its explanatory power could be said to rest on the imprecise and vague formulation of its constituent terms. Hence, to counter such objection, it is essential to specify more precisely the elements which are integral to the circumstances and situations which encourage the spread of organizational democracy.

The forces which underlie *international* variations are not a central concern of this monograph, but they include diversities in governmental and legislative initiatives, in the institutionalized structure of industrial relations, in the strategies and power of the main parties, and ideological and cultural conditions in the 'larger' society. Moreover, changes in a given country over a *period of time* are interrelated with varied legislative provisions, the economic cycle, and fluctuating managerial policies and modes of trade union organization and action in the firm. Additionally, a *spatial* analysis of variations requires the analyst to focus on distinctive configurations in economic 'infrastructural' conditions, in managerial strategies and 'styles', in industrial relations 'climate' in the firm, and in the policies of relevant employee collectivities.

A further refinement of the variables is necessary in order to carry out a more specific explanation of the origins and development of profit-sharing and employee-shareholding schemes. Moreover, to group the relevant factors in a way which is in accord with ongoing theoretical debates requires the specification of two main frameworks. The first (model A) is essentially *structuralist* in compass and is based on the assumption that the varying rates and patterns of adoption of profit sharing and employee shareholding stem from a combination of: (1) favourable governmental and legislative measures; and (2) economic 'infrastructural' differences. Governmental and legislative supports may be either facilitative or mandatory. And diverse economic 'infrastructural' conditions include the differences in legal status of publicly quoted and private companies, size and capital–labour ratio, the segmentation of labour and labour markets, varied rates of growth of enterprises, the rise of financial sector firms, and the decline of those in manufacturing and the new technologies.

In a second approach (model B), although the *constraining* influence of these wider structural conditions on action is fully acknowledged, emphasis is placed on the considerable measure of *choice* in the decision on whether or not to adopt schemes in the first place. These choices, however, are not entirely random and can be predicted from: (1) overall managerial strategies and 'styles' in industrial relations; (2) the industrial relations 'climate' of the firm; and (3) the power and attitudes of other organized groups. More specifically, consultative and paternal 'styles' of industrial relations management, the existence of other organizational democracy practices, and the strategies of trade unions and staff associations are all presumed to impact upon actual outcomes.

Turning to the empirical conclusions of this inquiry two basic issues are uppermost. First, what evidence is available to shed light on the overall theoretical approaches to employee financial participation and to the more general theme of organizational democracy itself? And, second, what are the principal findings with respect to the 'structuralist' and 'action' models which have been deployed to explain the varying patterns of adoption of profit-sharing and shareholding schemes?

In this monograph, it has, of course, not been our aim to test the general theory of organizational democracy. Indeed, in the more specific respect of profit sharing and employee shareholding, it has not been possible to examine all the relevant analytical dimensions and variables. Moreover, the international data presented have been largely descriptive and the few isolated findings of relevance to the main explanatory propositions have been largely confined to the experience of the USA. But so far as Britain is concerned, we have been able to conduct a brief temporal analysis of the main patterns of movement to supplement the main spatial analysis.

The changes in Britain over time were evaluated, partly by way of a brief historical account of the main movements and partly by reference to Inland Revenue statistics, to the WIRS 1 and WIRS 2 surveys, and to the Department of Employment-commissioned research. Our main conclusion is that there is a difference between the circumstances which were favourable to the early expansion of profit sharing and the modern advance centred around the Inland Revenue-approved schemes. Hence, the periods of growth in profit sharing in the nineteenth and early twentieth centuries were related to buoyant economic conditions, 'philanthropic' management policies, an expansion in trade union density, and considerable industrial unrest. Eras of diminished interest in profit sharing were typically associated with downswings in the economy and retrenchment on the part of labour. Moreover, it should be stressed that 'cyclical' theories were by no means inaccurate as a depiction of the oscillating patterns of advance and decay associated with the formative years of the movement.

But the modern progression of profit sharing and employee shareholding must be traced to rather different conditions. The period since 1979 witnessed a recession which was sharper in its effects upon trade unionism and strike activity than at any period since the 1930s. Yet, on the basis of the assumptions of a cyclical theory, a *decline* in profit-sharing and employee-shareholding schemes would have been anticipated.

To explain recent developments, the favourable legislation contained in the 1978, 1980, and 1984 Finance Acts is obviously important. However, there is at the same time a highly uneven pattern of advance that may be traced to a number of interconnected patterns of industrial relations institutions and policies in Britain. To begin with, managements advocating consultative approaches to their employees will tend to encourage a variety of employee-involvement practices, such as joint consultation, information, and profit sharing and share ownership. Moreover, the weaker position of the trade unions has ensured that managers have been able to promote *these* forms of involvement rather than being constrained to accept, say, extensions of collective bargaining or board-level union representation. In addition, the effects of the recession have been far from uniform and have been complicated by the advent of the new technologies and by the increasingly diverse experiences of those in employment. There are two main consequences. First, although the *macro* context differs from the earlier periods of advance of employee financial participation, at the *micro* level, it is in the expanding and larger publicly quoted companies that profit sharing and share ownership is being particularly developed. And, second, the 'human capital' requirements of the new technologies being adopted in the growth sectors of the economy encourage managements to seek to retain the workforce through profit sharing and share ownership and other modes of employee involvement.

But it is with respect to a *spatial* analysis of intersector and intercompany variations in adoption of schemes that the survey and case-study data permit a sharper and more discriminatory set of conclusions. The overall argument of this study has been that a model based on 'action' assumptions is the most satisfactory way of understanding the diverse patterns of development of schemes. Once again, this explains outcomes in terms of the choices of strategically placed decision makers who are constrained but not determined by the broader effects of the environment (and particularly by legislative provisions and economic 'infrastructural' forces). Moreover these choices are seen to be informed by various strategies and 'styles' adopted by the key decision makers, by the overall industrial relations 'climate' in the firm, and by the strategies of organized groups, such as trade unions.

In our view, the alternative structural model is unsatisfactory

The origins of economic democracy

on both theoretical and empirical counts. Theoretically, it is implausible that the attitudes and behaviour of the actual members of given organizations will have no consequences whatsoever on whether or not *company*-level practices will or will not be adopted. And empirically, not only is there a lack of consistency amongst the main structural variables, but it is clear that only part of the variance in actual practices can be explained by broader political and economic variables alone. Moreover, the use of case-study material has enabled us to identify a series of elements which are consequential in shaping actual decisions on whether or not to adopt schemes and to demonstrate the considerable significance of managerial strategy and 'style' and industrial relations climate in the firm.

Indeed, so far as a *spatial* analysis of variations in practice is concerned, it is arguable that the impact of government and the legislature is relatively limited. As we have seen, there is almost certainly a strong influence of facilitative legislation in accounting for international differences and the temporal changes in patterns of adoption of schemes in particular nations. But at any specific point in time, most firms are identically placed with respect to legislation and yet only some will have introduced schemes. To be sure, legislation may be framed in a way which makes it more suitable to some types of firms rather than others. And, indeed, there is evidence from both the survey and case-study phases of the research that publicly quoted rather than private companies find Inland Revenue-approved share-based schemes for employees far easier to establish. Moreover, as we have seen, it is reasonable to argue that firms with high capital–labour ratios are the most likely to develop arrangements which will be attractive to employees and yet will not run the gauntlet of Investment Protection Committee rulings or shareholder opposition. But the pronounced differences which remain (and not least amongst firms in a common category) suggest that we must look elsewhere for much of the explanation of the diverse patterns of adoption of schemes.

The economic 'infrastructure' thesis is, as we have seen, premised on a materialist theory of relationships at work in which the objective characteristics of companies rather than, say, 'styles' of industrial relations management are viewed as crucial. In this particular study, it was not possible to assess all the variables which are relevant to a materialist theory, but it was feasible to focus on the effects of enterprise size, the diverse rates of growth of particular companies, and industrial sector. So far as enterprise size is concerned, information was obtained on capital assets, annual turnover, multi- or single-establishment status of the firm, and enterprise autonomy. Growth was measured by trends in the workforce and in business volume. And the effects of industrial sector were established by classifying firms according to whether their principal activities were concerned with manufacturing, services, retail/distribution, finance, or some 'other' activity.

Of all the structural characteristics of companies, capital assets and annual turnover were found to be the best predictors of whether or not schemes had been adopted. Trends in business volume were also linked with the propensity to introduce profit sharing, and firms in the finance sector rather than in manufacturing of services were particularly likely to have introduced schemes. But establishment autonomy and trends in the workforce were not found to be generally related to the varying propensity to adopt schemes in British companies.

The patterning of data revealed by a structural analysis also reinforced the case for disaggregating the dependent variable. The thrust of the economic 'infrastructure' thesis (that large firms in the financial sector experiencing an increase in the workforce and in business volume are most likely to have developed schemes) applies most to APS schemes. The primary reason for this is the considerable propensity of firms in the financial sector to have adopted APS schemes. And this is, in turn, because of: (1) competitive labour market conditions; (2) the profitability of finance sector firms; (3) employee characteristics; and (4) knowledge and information on schemes. In the case of SAYE schemes, however, although the effects of capital assets and, above all, annual turnover are very strong, there is no relationship between the presence of a firm in the financial sector and the propensity to have introduced this specific form of employee shareholding. And this is because SAYE schemes do not have the same incentive effect as APS schemes for employees to remain in a given firm, not least because only a minority will typically commit themselves to a SAYE share-option contract.

But notwithstanding the undoubted significance of a number of economic 'infrastructural' variables, the importance of taking into account the choices of key personnel was underscored by the empirical analysis. To be sure, in the long run, it may be the case that if the intersectoral differences in employment prospects remain, certain structural variables will gradually assume a 'determining' character. This could conceivably apply, for instance, in the finance sector where competitive labour market conditions may increasingly place pressure on all the relevant managements to develop some arrangements for employee financial participation. And, indeed, it is arguable that choice is greatest at the earliest phases of development of given practices rather than at a later stage when processes of institutionalization (allied with competitive pressures) have made them almost universally applicable.

However, at present, there is no doubt that managerial strategies and 'styles' in industrial relations are relevant to understanding the varied rates of adoption of profit-sharing and employee-shareholding schemes. On the basis of case-study data, the primary objectives of managements in introducing schemes would appear to revolve around: (1) moral commitment; (2) staff retention; (3) employee involvement; (4) improved industrial relations performance; and (5) protection against takeover. In particular, the aim to make the staff more interested or involved was found to be prominent amongst the recalled motives of key respondents for adopting a scheme in the first place.

There is no doubt, too, that the 'styles' of industrial relations management in the company are significantly related to the introduction of most types of profit sharing and employee shareholding. For the purposes of this inquiry, the different 'styles' were assessed in the 'first-stage' survey by a series of questions eliciting information on the extent to which either 'consultative' or 'paternal' approaches to employee relations were prominent in particular companies. And, indeed, the composite measures assessing both these 'styles' were shown to be significantly related to the adoption of most forms of employee financial participation. The one exception was again APS schemes (the principal reason being once more the link between the finance sector and schemes of this type).

Furthermore, the overall industrial relations climate of the firm was also found to be connected with the propensity to adopt schemes. In recent years, the development of flexible organizational profiles and the encouragement of a considerable degree of employee involvement in decision making have been widely canvassed in managerial circles. And, on the basis of the survey data presented in this volume, there is undoubtedly a relationship between the presence of schemes for employee financial participation and: (1) the preference for reaching decisions on industrial relations issues by consultation or agreement; and (2) the existence of other channels of employee involvement in the firm. This pattern is also indicative of a coterminous relationship between several forms of economic and industrial democracy in contemporary Britain.

Hence, in the survey stage of the research, respondents were asked to what extent a series of decisions on industrial relations and financial issues were typically taken by management alone, after consultation, or after agreement/negotiation. It was found that there was a clear tendency for firms in which management shared decision making to be particularly prone to have adopted one or other of the main forms of all-employee shareholding scheme. However, although employee participation in industrial relations decisions was connected with the introduction of profit-sharing and share-ownership schemes, this linkage did not apply to involvement in financial-type issues. Furthermore, the case studies also revealed that it was common for employee financial participation to have stemmed from an overall policy in the firm to stimulate various forms of employee involvement.

Details were also obtained on the existence of participatory practices in companies and factor analysis revealed two broad clusters of arrangement that referred to trade union and non-trade union channels of representation respectively. Companies with machinery for joint consultation, formal and informal collective bargaining, regular meetings between supervisors and workgroups and management committees with employee or union representation, quality circles, and so on were shown to be the most likely to have adopted the main types of all-employee schemes for employee financial participation (APS schemes once again being the exception).

But while a participatory decision-making climate in the firm is related to the adoption of schemes, few relationships were discovered with payment systems. Perhaps not surprisingly, the existence of plant-wide bonuses in the firm proved to be an exception. Nevertheless, this overall finding is of considerable consequence for current debates on the origins and development of schemes, not least because, in public debates, some of the most prominent arguments have assumed a relationship of schemes with flexible patterns of remuneration and reward and with profit-related pay. Nevertheless, our findings suggest that policies of this type are *not* of major salience in convincing British managements to introduce schemes in the first place and that a 'broader' policy for stimulating employee involvement is a far more important consideration.

In any comprehensive examination of the origins and development of profit sharing and share ownership, the perceptions and actions of employee collectivities (and particularly trade unions) are also of considerable interest. The central conclusions of this study in these respects are as follows. First of all, the fears of the Webbs and other classical theorists of the labour movement that profit sharing is adverse to trade unionism and collective bargaining would seem to be largely unfounded. Indeed, in the early eras of advance, profit sharing flourished alongside expanding trade unionism. And in the survey research reported in this study, even though the linkage was probably indirect, a significant positive relationship was found between the presence of trade unions in the firm and the adoption of schemes. To be sure, on the basis of the evidence derived from interviews, the support of full-time union officers and lay representatives for most forms of employee financial participation would appear to be cautious and qualified. And there was detectable union opposition to ESO schemes. But, in general, it was found that so long as the all-employee schemes did not encroach upon collective bargaining, union officials by and large supported them.

Moreover, on the broader issue of collective representation, it is important to note that the presence of staff associations in the firm was a strong predictor of the presence of schemes. The case studies suggested that this relationship was seldom direct (though in one instance in particular, the introduction of a scheme did stem from the issue being raised first in a staff association meeting). But the main reason for this linkage appeared to be that the development of staff associations is connected with *both* consultative and paternal 'styles' of industrial relations management, and that these are, in turn, supportive to profit-sharing and employee-shareholding schemes. And at all events, the results indicated the importance of taking into account the existence and motives of the various forms of employee collectivity in any broad-ranging explanation of the origins and development of employee financial participation.

The upshot was overwhelming support for the general thesis of 'favourable conjunctures' for interpreting the advance of organizational and economic democracy and for an 'action' approach to understanding the more specific forces involved. Of course, this is not to deny the significance of external governmental supports or the considerable saliency of such economic 'infrastructural' factors as enterprise size, trends in business volume, and the financial sector. But these provide a series of constraints or opportunities for managements, trade unions, and employees to embark upon programmes for profit sharing and share ownership and they are not ultimately determinants of action itself. On the contrary, as we have seen, the choice of whether or not to embark upon schemes is fundamentally affected by managerial strategies and 'styles' in the human-resource field, by the overall industrial relations climate of the firm, and by the presence and policies of employee collectivities. Furthermore, the effects of any given variable do not always apply across all the main types of employee financial participation. This suggests not only the importance of differentiating between the main types of scheme but also that economic and organizational democracy are highly complex phenomena which require sophisticated multivariate explanations of their origins and development.

The results presented in this inquiry also indicate that a measure of cautious optimism is reasonable so far as the prospects for an expansion of schemes in the future are concerned. The favourable legislation on employee financial participation in Britain is unlikely to be repealed by a change in government and, indeed, it may well be extended to make the current provisions more adaptable to the requirements of private companies. Moreover, on the basis of the evidence of a steady expansion of approved schemes in the 1980s, the legislation appears to have provided a lasting inducement for companies to promote profit sharing and employee shareholding. Competitive economic pressures in certain employment sectors are ensuring that Inland Revenue-approved schemes are becoming progressively more widespread and employers have gradually been introducing *more* forms of profit sharing and employee shareholding. Facing the challenge of rapid technological and industrial change, a wide range of managements have cultivated either consultative or sophisticated paternal 'styles' in their approach to the workforce and have sought, as a matter of policy, to secure the commitment of employees to the firm as a whole. And these departures are all conducive to the advance of employee financial participation. Again, the broad consensus of informed opinion is that employee involvement should be stimulated as part of the overall industrial climate of the firm and, as we have seen, this is undoubtedly a favourable backcloth for the advance of profit-sharing and shareholding schemes. Furthermore, the trade unions are unlikely to act as any major brake on the advance of all-employee schemes.

But there is another issue of fundamental importance which arises whenever the issue of the financial participation of employees in the enterprise is discussed. And this is: how effective are schemes in actual practice in occasioning improvements in job satisfaction, productivity, the acceptance by employees of profitability as a corporate objective, the reduction of conflict and tension at work, and so on? Having outlined the main factors affecting the development of schemes, it is appropriate to move on, to assess in depth and detail, the *consequences* of the introduction of schemes in the firm. And this is, of course, precisely the objective of the forthcoming volume.

Appendix one

Employee financial participation in Britain: regression and discriminant analysis

It has been shown that employee financial participation in Britain is a highly complex phenomenon. It is thus valuable to attempt to rank more precisely the effects of the main independent variables and to assess their predictive power.

Up to a point, the correlation techniques used in the study enable the analyst to show the strength of relationships and they also provide a guide to the relative explanatory importance of given variables. But supplementary regression analysis is useful in order to rank more precisely the effects of each variable. However, in order to avoid the considerable data loss occasioned by using factors (and this applied particularly to the composite variable assessing the presence of trade union-type participation bodies in the firm), the results presented are based on a selected number of variables and should be regarded as illustrative rather than conclusive.

Regression analysis

In table A.1 the results of the multiple regression for the *generally based* (i.e. all-employee schemes) are set out. It will be seen that five variables alone yield a multiple r of 0.66 and a value of r^2 of 0.43. Ranking the variables in descending order according to their relative explanatory strength reveals the following pattern:

1. *Staff associations*: the presence of staff associations is strongly associated with firms adopting generally based profit-sharing and shareholding schemes.

2. *Financial sector*: firms in the financial sector are clearly the most likely to have adopted a variety of programmes for employee financial participation.

3. *Capital assets*: the largest firms are clearly the most likely to adopt generally based profit-sharing and shareholding schemes.

4. *Non-union-type participation bodies*: firms practising employee participation through non-union channels are particularly likely to have generally based schemes.

5. *Paternalism*: support for a decision-making 'style' in which employees are viewed as an integral part of the company favours profit sharing and share ownership.

It was also noted that, in the case of the enterprise variables, *a high level of capital assets is crucial*. Indeed, a series of further highly significant relationships isolated in the earlier analysis, such as trends in business volume and annual turnover, are clearly related to the scale of the enterprise. Moreover, the regression analysis does reveal that a series of *industrial relations variables* are of considerable consequence. Certainly the presence of staff associations, the existence of other non-union-type participation channels, and support for paternalism are relevant to the adoption of all-employee schemes for profit sharing and share ownership.

Table A.1 The strength and rank of the main influences on the adoption of generally based (i.e. all-employee) schemes for profit sharing or share ownership

Variable	Multiple r	r²	Correlation	β
1 Staff association	0.54	0.29	0.54	0.54
2 Enterprise in financial sector	0.62	0.38	0.25	0.30
3 Higher rather than lower capital assets	0.64	0.41	0.43	0.19
4 Presence of non-union-type participation bodies	0.65	0.42	0.26	0.11
5 Support for paternalism	0.66	0.43	0.22	0.10

Note: The data are based on multiple regression analysis. Because of missing data the correlations are slightly but not typically nor markedly different from those presented in other tables. Variables occasioning considerable data loss (and notably the presence of trade union-type participative bodies in the firm) were omitted from the analysis.

Discriminant analysis

To obtain a more precise ranking of the variables associated with the decisions in companies to embark on various programmes for employee financial participation, discriminant analysis is also a valuable technique. Again, it reveals the substantial differences between Inland Revenue-approved profit-sharing (APS) schemes and save as you earn (SAYE) schemes. Discriminant analysis is essentially a predictive technique by which linear combinations of independent – sometimes called predictor – variables are formed. These provide the basis of classifying cases into one group or

Table A.2 Discriminant analysis: pooled-within-groups correlations of independent (predictor) variables and types of profit sharing or share ownership

General scheme (i.e. all-employee)			Any scheme			Inland Revenue-approved profit-sharing (APS) scheme			Save as you earn (SAYE) scheme		
0.71	1	Presence of staff association in enterprise	0.66	1	Presence of staff association in enterprise	0.70	1	Enterprise in financial sector	0.88	1	Presence of staff association in enterprise
0.53	2	Higher rather than lower capital assets	0.64	2	Higher rather than lower capital assets	0.66	2	Higher rather than lower capital assets	0.66	2	Higher rather than lower annual turnover
0.45	3	Higher rather than lower annual turnover	0.60	3	Higher rather than lower annual turnover	0.36	3	Higher rather than lower annual turnover	0.43	3	Higher rather than lower capital assets
0.28	4	Presence of non-union-type participation bodies	0.40	4	Presence of non-union-type participation bodies	0.34	4	Presence of staff association in enterprise	0.38	4	Multi- rather than single establishment
0.27	5	Multi- rather than single establishment	0.35	5	Multi- rather than single establishment	0.33	5	Extent of increase in business volume	0.36	5	Presence of union in enterprise
0.25	6	Presence of union-based participation bodies	0.30	6	Presence of union in enterprise	-0.11	6	Presence of union in enterprise	0.34	6	Presence of union-based participation bodies
0.25	7	Enterprise in financial sector	0.25	7	Presence of union-based participation bodies	0.09	7	Multi- rather than single establishment	0.26	7	Presence of non-union-type participation bodies
0.25	8	Presence of union in enterprise	0.25	8	Enterprise in financial sector	-0.06	8	Presence of union-based participation bodies	0.08	8	Extent of increase in business volume
0.19	9	Extent of increase in business volume	0.23	9	Extent of increase in business volume	-0.04	9	Presence of non-union-type participation bodies	0.02	9	Enterprise in financial sector

another in a binary combination (in this instance the adoption or
non-adoption of various schemes for profit sharing and employee
shareholding). The technique enables the analyst both to identify
the importance of each independent variable and to discover how
well the variables are able to predict outcomes.

In table A.2, the results of a discriminant analysis based on
nine key independent variables are set out. Taking, first of all,
then, the adoption of *any generally based* scheme for profit sharing
or share ownership, discriminant analysis enables a ranking of the
importance of the main explanatory variables as follows: presence
of staff association in enterprise, higher rather than lower capital
assets, higher rather than lower annual turnover, multi- rather
than single establishment, presence of non-union-type participation
bodies, presence of union-based participation bodies, enterprise in
financial sector, presence of union in enterprise, and extent of
increase in business volume. Moreover, the pooled-within-groups
correlations clearly give a rough indication of the *magnitude* of
importance of each independent variable and reveal the particular
saliency of the presence of a staff association, a high level of
capital assets, and a large annual turnover.

The distinctive pattern of influences on the adoption of Inland
Revenue-approved profit-sharing (APS) schemes revealed in the
main report is reinforced by discriminant analysis. By far the most
important factors associated with the adoption of these types of
scheme are the enterprise being in the financial sector and having
higher rather than lower capital assets. The only other variables of
any consequence are a higher rather than lower annual turnover,
the presence of staff associations, and the extent of increase in
business volume. Firms without unions are shown to be more
likely than those with such bodies to embark upon APS schemes.
Moreover, the presence of additional participation channels
(whether union- or non-union-based) is irrelevant to the adoption
of the APS programme.

Of further interest, too, is to examine the save as you earn
(SAYE) schemes in a little more detail. The pattern of influences
does not differ markedly from that obtaining for adoption of any
generally based scheme, but there are still some distinctive aspects
to the rank order of the variables and to the magnitude of the
correlations in this particular case. To begin with, then, the
presence of staff associations is of special importance to the SAYE
group, as is a higher rather than lower annual turnover. Most of
the industrial relations variables have a middling rank order
amongst the explanatory forces. Importantly, too, whether or not
the enterprise is in the financial sector is largely *irrelevant* to

Table A.3 Classification of 'grouped' cases using discriminant analysis

	Actual group	Number of cases	Predicted group membership 0	Predicted group membership 1	Percentage of 'grouped' cases classified correctly	After-case selection (50% sample)
General scheme						
Group No	0	88	71 (80.7%)	17 (19.3%)	80.9	81.4
Group Yes	1	163	31 (19.0%)	132 (81.0%)		
Any scheme						
Group No	0	63	51 (81.0%)	12 (19.0%)	74.9	74.4
Group Yes	1	188	51 (27.1%)	137 (72.9%)		
Inland Revenue-approved profit-sharing (APS) scheme						
Group No	0	194	138 (71.1%)	56 (28.9%)	70.1	68.2
Group Yes	1	57	19 (33.3%)	38 (66.7%)		
Save as you earn (SAYE) scheme						
Group No	0	150	116 (77.3%)	34 (22.7%)	80.9	80.6
Group Yes	1	101	14 (13.9%)	87 (86.1%)		

Note: 303 cases processed; 2 cases excluded for missing or out-of-range group codes; 52 cases had at least one missing discriminant function; 251 cases were used.

the adoption of SAYE schemes. *Indeed, financial sector is at exactly the opposite end in the rank order of the group of variables associated with the introduction of APS and SAYE schemes respectively.*

Table A.3 incorporates the findings on the *classification of outcomes.* Discriminant analysis enables a comparison to be made between actual group membership (i.e. the firm having a given profit-sharing or share-ownership scheme) and that predicted on the basis of our selected group of explanatory variables. Moreover, a high percentage of correctly classified cases suggests that our particular group of explanatory variables is indeed central to the adoption of profit-sharing or share-ownership schemes in companies in Britain. To make the analysis more genuinely predictive, and to guard against the problem of a loss of data having an effect on the results, a random 50 per cent sample of cases was also selected (the outcome was found to be very similar to that obtaining for the larger group; see again table A.3).

Taking first of all the firms having any generally based (i.e. all-employee) scheme, of the 163 which had profit-sharing or share-ownership arrangements of this type, 132 were identified correctly by our particular group of explanatory variables. Moreover, the overall percentage of cases correctly classified was an impressively high 80.9 per cent (203 out of 251 companies). For *any* schemes and particularly the Inland Revenue-approved profit-sharing (APS) schemes the overall percentages of 'grouped' cases correctly classified (at 74.9 per cent and 70.1 per cent respectively) were somewhat less satisfactory. In the latter instance, this particularly reflects the limited saliency of the industrial relations variables. But for the save as you earn (SAYE) schemes there was again a very high percentage of cases correctly classified (80.9 per cent).

In sum, then, discriminant analysis proved to be a useful technique for isolating the main forces associated with the adoption of profit-sharing and share-ownership schemes in companies in Britain. Above all, it facilitated a more precise ranking and weighting of the key influences identified from correlation and regression techniques. And it also enabled us to assess the predictive power of the key explanatory variables, while demonstrating the radically different origins of APS and SAYE schemes respectively.

119

Appendix two

Technical details, sample, and sampling procedures

At a number of points in the text, brief details of the sample were presented and, whenever it was important to do so, the wording of the questions from which the data were derived was also included. However, in appendix 2 and appendix 3, there is an attempt to set out, in a more comprehensive and focused form, the methods, the relevant information on sampling, and the interview schedules. In the text, there was no neat division between stage 1 (survey) and stage 2 (case studies) material. On the contrary, an integration of the two sets of data seemed to us to be the most fruitful way to present the evidence which was available. None the less, for reasons of simplicity and economy, it is sensible to outline the survey details here, leaving the background information on the case studies for the relevant appendix in the second volume.

In the technical appendix, details are set out on: (1) sampling; (2) response rates; (3) sample characteristics; (4) respondent identification; and (5) weighting procedures.

Sampling

The sampling frame for publicly quoted companies was the *Stock Exchange Yearbook*. This was used in conjunction with a listing of publicly quoted companies which have any type of share-incentive or share-option scheme. The listing is published by Extel and is compiled from an examination of companies' annual reports. Companies included in the list were oversampled in order to improve the pick-up of companies with schemes. Analysis was weighted to correct for this oversampling. Privately owned companies were drawn from Jordan's *Britain's Top Private Companies – the first 2000*, covering companies with a turnover in excess of £¾ million. In addition, a small subgroup of major foreign-owned firms, not quoted on the stock exchange, was drawn from the *Times Top 1000* and from a listing provided by the Japanese Chamber of Commerce.

A total of 1,300 companies were drawn from these sources distributed as follows:

	Addresses issued	Screening quotas
Extel	600	450
Other: *Stock Exchange Yearbook* and foreign firms	300	200
Jordan's Directory	400	200

Interviewers were then required to carry out short 'screening' interviews with a set quota of companies from each sample source. These quotas are shown on the right-hand side of the table above. A screening interview involved establishing: (1) the number of employees in the enterprise; (2) the existence of profit sharing; and (3) the extent of schemes (i.e. number and type of employees covered). The screening interview led to a full interview, conducted either face-to-face or by telephone, if it fitted the interview quota set. These quotas were arrived at by splitting the sample into the three 'interest segments' itemized below. The target numbers and numbers of interviews achieved for each segment are also shown. There was a serious shortfall in the number of type B interviews; companies falling into this category were far rarer than had originally been envisaged and it was impossible to make up their number. Given that less full interviews were conducted, it was decided to increase the extent of the screening exercise from 850 to over 1,100.

	Target interviews	Achieved
A Enterprise with APS or SAYE share-option schemes	150 face-to-face interviews	156
B Enterprise with non-exempt general employee scheme	50 face-to-face interviews with those having share schemes or those with cash schemes who had considered an exempt scheme	13
	125 telephone interviews with those having cash schemes who had not considered an exempt scheme	22
C Enterprise with no general employee scheme	100 telephone interviews	112

121

Response rates

The table below shows the number of contacts made and their outcome. A total of 1,125 successful contacts – successful in that either a screening interview or full interview took place as a result – were made. The main reasons for failed contacts were refusals and unavailability. The response rate calculated on the number of eligible contacts, excluding company closures and referrals, is 1,125/1,380, that is, 82 per cent.

	Total	Mfg	Industry Service	Retail	Finance	Other
Base: Total contacts	1423	590	165	391	143	134
	No.	No.	No.	No.	No.	No.
Interview	303	145	29	59	45	25
Screening only	822	341	103	243	68	67
Failed screening:						
Refusals	164	52	20	54	16	22
Breakdown during interview	6	3	–	–	3	–
Not available within deadline	89	37	12	23	4	13
Company closed down/change of ownership	11	2	1	4	1	3
Referred elsewhere	28	10	–	8	6	4

Note: Interviewing was carried out by fully trained interviewers of IFF Research Ltd and took place in May and early June 1985.

Sample characteristics

The composition of the 1,125 screened establishments and of the 303 establishments which went on to a full interview is given below:

	Establishments screened	Establishments interviewed
	1125	303
	No.	No.
Publicly quoted:	574	224
large[a]	419	174
small[b]	155	50
Privately owned:	512	74
large	126	26
small	386	48
Foreign owned	39	5

Manufacturing	486	145
Service	132	29
Retail/distribution	302	59
Finance	113	45
Other	92	25

Note: ªLarge is defined as having a turnover of over £10m; ᵇsmall is defined as having a turnover of £10m or less.

Respondent identification

The respondent for the survey was defined as the person most involved in setting up schemes (where schemes existed) or who would know about the company's policies with regard to profit sharing and share ownership. The approach used to identify the most appropriate respondent was to speak to the company secretary or financial director, describe the subject of the study to them, and ask them who the most appropriate respondent would be. In the majority of cases, they answered the questions themselves.

Job titles	*All screened* 1125	*All interviewed* 303
	%	%
Company secretary	50	57
Finance director/controller	10	14
Group finance director	1	1
Personnel manager/director	3	5
Assistant/deputy company secretary	5	8
Managing director	4	1
Director/senior executive	3	1
Other	6	7
Not stated (either company secretary or financial director)	17	7

Weighting procedures

In order to restore the sample's representativeness of the survey population (given that firms with schemes had been oversampled), counts were carried out to establish the profile of enterprises listed in each of the sample sources used. These counts produced the matrix given below and the enterprises sampled in each cell were then weighted to meet these targets.

Turnover	Privately owned	Enterprises Publicly quoted Extel	Other
Less than £3½m	1767	32	387
£3½–10m	1615	90	291
£11–99m	606	346	358
£100–499m	⎫	130	70
	12		
£500m+	⎭	111	35
Total	4000	709	1141

Note: Plus foreign owned with weight of 1.

The resulting weighting factors were as follows:

	Privately owned	Publicly quoted Extel	Other
Less than £3½m	11.40	1.88	9.00
£3½–10m	6.99	1.87	6.19
£11–99m	5.32	2.19	4.65
£100–499m	⎫	1.40	5.38
	1.00		
£500m+	⎭	1.66	3.18

Appendix three

The questionnaires

In this volume, questionnaires from the screening interviews and the 'main-stage' survey are set out. Because the schedules used were highly complex and lengthy only part of the material is presented and covers: (1) the screening questionnaire; (2) the questionnaire for firms with an Inland Revenue-approved profit-sharing (APS) scheme; and (3) the questionnaire for firms with *no* generally based schemes. Additional information (similar in type to the APS questionnaire) was obtained to cover the situations of: (1) cash-based profit sharing; (2) SAYE schemes; and (3) *non-approved* share-ownership schemes. However, most of the questions asked to assess these types of scheme were identical to those in the APS questionnaire but adapted to the type concerned. Moreover, the background questions were asked in *all* 'main-stage' companies regardless of type of scheme or whether or not the firm had any all-employee scheme for profit sharing at all. Hence, the material presented does provide a very considerable coverage of the items included in the survey stage. In the forth-coming volume, the case-study schedules are included and cover: (1) interviews with key respondents; (2) interviews with trade union officials; and (3) the employee-attitudes questionnaire.

Screening questionnaire (omitting most codes and most interviewer instructions)

SHARE-OWNERSHIP AND PROFIT-SHARING SCHEMES SCREENING QUESTIONNAIRE

STICK ADDRESS LABEL HERE		OUTCOME	
Sample Source		*Personal interview* – type **A**	1
		– type **B**	2
Extel	1	Telephone interview (1)	3
Stock Exchange Yearbook	2	Telephone interview (2)	4
Jordan's	3 or 4	Positive screening only	5
American owned	5	Breakdown during interview	7
Japanese owned	6	Not available within deadline	8
		Unobtainable	9
		Other	X

CONTACT RECORD (Please complete for every contact, however short)

CONTACT NO.	DATE	TIME	SPOKE TO	OUTCOME
1				
2				
3				
4				

ASK TELEPHONIST
Is that ....(COMPANY) of ....(ADDRESS)?
Could you put me through to the company secretary or finance director?
NAME ....
FULL JOB TITLE ....

INTRODUCTION
Good morning/afternoon. I am...........from IFF Research Ltd. We are carrying out a study on behalf of the Department of Employment. It is about *employee share-ownership and profit-sharing schemes*, and we are particularly interested in speaking to someone who would know about your company's policies with regard to such schemes.

1a Are you the most appropriate person to speak to about this?

Yes . . . .

No . . . .

1b Who should I speak to?

NAME . . . .

JOB TITLE . . . .

2 Does . . . . (ENTERPRISE NAME) or any subsidiary or division of the company operate profit-sharing or share-ownership schemes of any kind?

Yes . . . .

No . . . .

3 Are any of the following types of scheme in operation within . . . . (ENTERPRISE NAME) in the UK?

READ OUT ITALIC SECTIONS: REST OF EXPLANATION CAN BE USED AS NECESSARY.

a) *Inland Revenue-approved profit-sharing scheme,* that is, a scheme whereby profit is allocated to a trust fund which acquires shares on behalf of employees. The employer does not pay income tax on the value of the shares, either when bought or sold on the employee's behalf (provided they are not sold for at least seven years).

b) *SAYE share-option scheme,* that is, a scheme whereby employees are given the option to buy a certain number of shares at a fixed price – the shares being bought from the proceeds of a SAYE savings contract. The employee does not have to pay any income tax on buying the shares at a favourable price or on any increase in the value of the shares.

c) *Other share-ownership scheme applying to all or most employees* but not Inland Revenue-approved, therefore no income tax relief attaches.

d) *Other share-ownership scheme for selected employees,* for example, directors, key executives, staff in certain divisions of the company, etc.

e) *Cash-based profit-sharing scheme for all or most employees.*

f) *Cash-based profit-sharing scheme for selected employees only.*

4 How many employees in total does the organization employ in the UK?

IF DON'T KNOW: Could you tell me *roughly* how many employees the organization has? WRITE IN ANSWER AND CODE BELOW:

WRITE IN [   ]

ASK Q5–8 FOR EACH SCHEME TYPE OPERATED

5a And how many are eligible for the ....NAME TYPE OF SCHEME?

5b How many participate in the ....NAME TYPE OF SCHEME?

6 Who is eligible for the scheme?
   READ OUT AND CODE BELOW

7 What is the necessary period of service, if any, before employees become eligible?

8 Does the scheme apply throughout the whole organization in the UK or only to certain companies/divisions?
   IF THERE IS MORE THAN ONE SCHEME WITHIN A *SCHEME TYPE* USE SPACE PROVIDED AND GIVE DETAILS.

	SCHEME TYPE					
	(a)	(b)	(c)	(d)	(e)	(f)
5a No. of employees eligible	⊞	⊞	⊞	⊞	⊞	⊞
5b No. participating	⊞	⊞	⊞	⊞	☐	☐

6 *Type of employee eligible*

	(a)	(b)	(c)	(d)	(e)	(f)
All/most full- and part-time employees (with certain period of service)	1	1	1	1	1	1
All/most full-time employees only (with certain period of service)	2	2	2	2	2	2
Directors and other selected executives	3	3	3	3	3	3
Directors only	4	4	4	4	4	4
Other (WRITE IN) __	0	0	0	0	0	0

_____

_____

7	*Necessary period of service*						
	5 years +	5	5	5	5	5	5
	4 years	4	4	4	4	4	4
	3 years	3	3	3	3	3	3
	2 years	2	2	2	2	2	2
	1 year or less	1	1	1	1	1	1
	None	0	0	0	0	0	0
8	*Extent*						
	Throughout whole organization	8	8	8	8	8	8
	Only to certain companies/divisions	9	9	9	9	9	9

COMMENTS _____

ASK ALL WHO OPERATE NEITHER A SAYE SCHEME NOR AN APPROVED SCHEME:
OTHERS SEE NOTE BELOW

9 Has your company ever considered implementing a SAYE scheme or an approved profit-sharing scheme based on the issue of shares?

Yes ....
No ....

Personal interviews, firms with an APS scheme

PROFIT-SHARING AND SHARE-OWNERSHIP SCHEMES

SECTION 1: INTRODUCTION

1 Did ....(ENTERPRISE NAME) ever have any other scheme(s) prior to your current ones?

Yes ....
No ....

2	*What type of scheme was it?*	Scheme:	1	2	3
	a) Inland Revenue-approved profit-sharing scheme		1	1	1
	SAYE share-option scheme		2	2	2
	Other share-ownership scheme				
	i) involving gift of shares		3	3	3
	ii) involving purchase of shares		4	4	4

129

The origins of economic democracy

Cash-based profit sharing	5	5	5
Other (WRITE IN) _____			
_____			
_____	V	V	V

b) *Did it apply to:*

The whole organization in the UK?	1	1	1

or

Only to certain divisions/companies?	2	2	2

c) *Who was eligible for the scheme?*

All full/part-time staff with certain period of service	1	1	1
All full-time staff within certain period of service	2	2	2
Directors/other senior executives	3	3	3
Directors only	4	4	4

d) *What was the necessary period of service before staff were eligible?*

5 years +	5	5	5
4 years	4	4	4
3 years	3	3	3
2 years	2	2	2
1 year or less	1	1	1
None	0	0	0

e) *When was the scheme discontinued?*   ☐☐ ☐☐ ☐☐

f) *Why was it discontinued?*

Change of legislation	1	1	1
Other (WRITE IN) _____			
_____			
_____	V	V	V

SECTION 2: APPROVED PROFIT-SHARING SCHEME

THIS SECTION APPLIES TO ALL
RESPONDENTS WITH TYPE A SCHEME
(A1, SCREENER).
OTHERS GO TO NEXT SECTION

I'd now like to run through the background to the introduction of your approved profit-sharing scheme:

3 When was it introduced?

WRITE IN YEAR _____

4 Was it a totally new scheme or a modification of an existing one?

New ...
Modification ...

5 What led to its introduction/the modification?
PROBE: Was it in response to external or internal events?
What events?
NOTE: IF INITIAL ANSWER IS 'management policy'
PROBE TO FIND OUT EXACTLY *HOW* IT
BECAME POLICY.

_____
_____
_____
_____
_____

6 What were seen to be the objectives of the scheme at this stage?
PROBE: What exactly was it hoped to achieve by this?

_____
_____
_____
_____

7 On this card are a number of aims which sometimes lie behind the introduction of such a scheme. Could you indicate how important each of these factors was in your case by rating them 1 to 5, where 5 is 'very important' and 1 'not at all important'?

	Very important				Not at all important
To make employees more profit conscious/more interested in the company's success	5	4	3	2	1
To increase employees' sense of commitment to the company/make staff more likely to stay	5	4	3	2	1
To act as an incentive for greater productivity	5	4	3	2	1
To make employees feel that they are part of the company – working *with* it, not just *for* it	5	4	3	2	1
To help hold wage claims down	5	4	3	2	1

131

To provide a tax-efficient
means of reward

i) for the employees	5	4	3	2	1
ii) for the company	5	4	3	2	1

To ensure that employees
benefit from the company's
profitability   5   4   3   2   1

To increase employees'
understanding of the
financial issues that
face the company   5   4   3   2   1

To increase the sense of co-
operation between management
and workforce   5   4   3   2   1

8a Who was consulted during this initial stage, that is, before the exact form of the scheme was finalized? READ OUT AND CODE BELOW

Board of Directors	1
Shareholders	2
Employees'/Workers' Representatives	3
Company solicitor	4
Registrars	5
Outside Consultants	6
Other (WRITE IN) _____	V

8b How were decisions made regarding the type of scheme chosen: Were they taken by *management alone*; by management alone but after asking the opinions of the workforce; taken by negotiation between management and representatives of the workforce?
REPEAT FOR EACH FACTOR
DECIDED BY ...

	Mgt alone	Mgt after consultation	Mgt in negotiation	N/A
i) the type of scheme chosen	1	2	3	0
ii) rules governing eligibility	1	2	3	0
iii) the level of funds to be allocated to the scheme	1	2	3	0
iv) the method of determining individual allocations	1	2	3	0

132

8c How favourable was the employees' response to the idea of the scheme being introduced?

> Not at all favourable 1
> Not very favourable 2
> Indifferent 3
> Fairly favourable 4
> Very favourable 5
> No response/don't know X

9 What initial research into the scheme was carried out, if any? PROBE: Were any other schemes considered? Any feasibility studies carried out?
DO NOT READ OUT. WRITE IN AND CODE BELOW.

> Formal evaluation of alternatives, for example, reports prepared 1
> 'Informal' evaluation of alternatives, for example, talking to other companies 2
> No alternatives considered 3
> Other (WRITE IN) _____
> _____ V

10 What do you think are the advantages of this scheme over:
a) A cash profit-sharing scheme?

> _____
> _____
> _____

b) A SAYE share-option scheme?

> _____
> _____
> _____

11a How long did it take between the idea being raised and the scheme actually being submitted for approval by the Inland Revenue?
> WRITE IN _____ (MONTHS)

11b What problems, if any, were encountered during this time?

> _____
> _____
> _____
> None ... 0

11c How long did Inland Revenue approval take?
> WRITE IN _____ (MONTHS)

11d Were there any problems in obtaining this?

> Yes ... 1
> No ... 2

133

The origins of economic democracy

DETAILS

_____
_____
_____

11e How helpful were the Inland Revenue?

Very helpful 1
Fairly helpful 2
Not very helpful 3
Not at all helpful 4

12a How do you decide the amount of profit to be allocated to the fund?

Fixed % of pre-tax
profits   1

% of profits decided
at directors'
discretion   2

% of profits beyond
a fixed threshold   3   What is the threshold?
                                    _____

Other (WRITE IN)

_____
_____   4

12b What type of shares are distributed to employees?
Are they ...

Voting – full voting rights 1
            – voting by proxy 2
Non-voting 3

13a And how are individual allocations determined?

Fixed rate 1
Sliding scale 2
Other (WRITE IN) ... V

13d What criteria are taken into account?

Salary 1
Grade/position in company 2
Age 3
Length of service 4
Individual performance 5
Other (WRITE IN) _____ V

14 i) What percentage of profit has been allocated in recent years?
    ii) What order of reward for employees has this resulted in?
        TRY TO OBTAIN A MEASURE IN TERMS OF % OF
        SALARY

i) % of profit   ii) % of salary

_____   _____
_____   _____
_____   _____

15 What happens to an employee's shares in the event of them
    leaving the organization to go to another job?
    WRITE IN

    _____
    _____
    _____
    _____
    _____

16a What is the minimum retention period for shares under your
    scheme?

                        2 years 1
                        3 years 2
                        4 years 3
                        5 years 4
                        6 years + ... 5

16b How many employees *opt* to sell their shares before the full
    tax-relief entitlement has accrued? That is, before they have
    held them for 7 years. CHECK WHETHER THE FIGURE
    GIVEN INCLUDES LEAVERS OR NOT; IF POSSIBLE
    OBTAIN SEPARATE FIGURES FOR LEAVERS VERSUS
    THOSE WHO CHOOSE TO SELL SHARES.

                        WRITE IN _____

17a How did you go about informing your employees about the
    scheme?
    READ OUT
                        Via standard Inland Revenue
                          booklet 1
                        Special company booklet 2
                        Memo 3
                        Video 4
                        Staff meetings 5
                        Via union channels 6
                        Other (WRITE IN) _____
                        _____ V

17b How much information were employees given beyond the
    basic facts? For example, were the company's objectives in
    introducing the scheme explained? How were they described?
    READ OUT

135

Mechanics of the scheme/how to
participate 1
Benefits of the scheme/why
employees should participate 2
Company's objectives in
introducing scheme 3
Other information (WRITE IN) _____
_____ V

18a How satisfied are you with the level of participation in the
scheme?

Very satisfied 5
Fairly satisfied 4
Neither satisfied nor dissatisfied 3
Not very satisfied 2
Not at all satisfied 1

18b ASK ALL: What do you attribute the level of participation
to?
PROBE: What are employees' attitudes to the scheme?
What type of employees are participating?

_____
_____
_____
_____

18c We sent a self-completion sheet to you requesting details of
eligibility and participation levels; do you have this available?
COLLECT AND CHECK THAT DETAILS ARE GIVEN
IN AN UNDERSTANDABLE FORM THEN ATTACH
FIRMLY TO QUESTIONNAIRE.
IF NOT COMPLETED, TRY TO COMPLETE BELOW,
EITHER IN NUMBERS, %, OR WORDS, OR ARRANGE
TO 'PHONE BACK FOR THE FIGURES.
DATE _____   TIME _____
DO NOT AGREE TO THE RESPONDENT POSTING
THE DETAILS BACK TO HEAD OFFICE

	Total no. of employees in workforce	Total no. eligible for scheme	Total no. participating in scheme
Total			
Type of employment:			
Full time			
Part time			

Grade of employee:

Unskilled manual			
Skilled manual			
General clerical			
Professional/technical			
Junior management			
Senior management			
Other (PLEASE SPECIFY)			

COMMENTS ON ABOVE

19a How successful has the scheme been in terms of the following objectives, on a scale of 1 to 5, where 5 is 'very successful' and 1 'not at all successful'?

	Very successful		Not at all successful			Don't know
A to make employees more profit conscious/more interested in the company's success	5	4	3	2	1	X
B to increase employees' sense of commitment to the company/make staff more likely to stay	5	4	3	2	1	X
C to act as an incentive for greater productivity	5	4	3	2	1	X
D to make employees feel that they are part of the company – working *with* it, not just *for* it	5	4	3	2	1	X
E to help hold wage claims down	5	4	3	2	1	X
F to provide a tax-efficient means of reward:						
i) for the employees	5	4	3	2	1	X
ii) for the company	5	4	3	2	1	X
G to ensure that employees benefit from the company's profitability	5	4	3	2	1	X

137

H to increase employees'
   understanding of the
   financial issues that face
   the company   5   4   3   2   1   X

I to increase the sense of
   co-operation between
   management and
   workforce   5   4   3   2   1   X

19b ASK OF ANY OBJECTIVE RATED 1 OR 2:
You feel the scheme has not been particularly successful in . . . . .
(NAME OBJECTIVE). Why do you think that is?
Objective

A	
B	
C	
D	
E	
F (i)	
F (ii)	
G	
H	
I	

20 What (other) problems, if any, have you encountered with the scheme?
PROBE: Are any changes envisaged as a result of this?

_____

_____
_____
_____

21a Do you have any estimate of the administrative costs involved:
  i) in setting up the scheme? _____
  ii) in running the scheme? _____

21b Can I just check what factors have been included in your estimate?

	Setting up	Running costs
New staff hired	1	1
Time spent by existing staff	2	2
Publication of leaflets	3	3
Legal fees	4	4
Other consultancy fees	5	5
Other (WRITE IN)		

_____

_____
_____

BACKGROUND ASK ALL:

70 What are your views on current share-ownership and profit-sharing legislation as it stands? PROBE: Would you like to see any amendments made or new legislation introduced?

                           Amendments needed 1

DETAILS   _____

                  _____

                  No amendments needed 2
                  Don't know X

71a Does _____ (ENTERPRISE NAME) have any plans for the introduction of any new schemes?

                                      Yes . . . 1

                                        No . . . 2

71b What types of scheme(s) are you planning to introduce?
             IR-approved profit-sharing scheme 1
             SAYE share-option scheme 2
              Executive share option 3

Other share-based scheme 4
Cash-based profit-sharing scheme – all
employees 5
Cash-based profit-sharing scheme – selected
employees 6
Other (WRITE IN) _____
_____ V

71c What led to these plans?

_____
_____
_____
_____

Can I just check on other types of employee involvement
which exist within your organization?:
72a Are any of the workforce members of:

Trade unions 1
Staff associations 2
Neither 0

72b Approximately what percentage of the workforce are trade
union or staff association members? (PROBE TO NEAREST
10%)

Total	TU	SA
%	%	%

73 Do all the *manual* workers in this organization normally have
to be members of a union in order to have or keep their jobs?
Yes – all 1
Not all, but some 2
No, none 3

74 Are there any of the following types of employee involvement
in your company?
Regular meetings between supervisors
and workgroups 1
Joint consultation/works council
committees 2
Job redesign involving employees or
their representatives 3
Productivity bargaining 4
Quality circles 5
New technology agreements 6

Formal collective bargaining 7
Informal collective bargaining 8
Management committees where there is
employee or union representation 9

75 Are the following types of decision in your company typically
taken by: (a) management alone; (b) management alone but
after asking the opinions of representatives of the workforce;
(c) taken by negotiation between management and representatives of the workforce?

	Manage-ment alone	After asking opinions	Negotia-tion	Not applic-able	Don't know
Wages and salaries	1	2	3	4	5
Safety and health	1	2	3	4	5
Discipline	1	2	3	4	5
Introduction of new technology	1	2	3	4	5
Shift or overtime working	1	2	3	4	5
Manning levels	1	2	3	4	5
Increase/reduction of the workforce	1	2	3	4	5
Investment in new units	1	2	3	4	5
How much of the companies profits should be put into additional wages and share dividends, and how much into investment	1	2	3	4	5

76 I am now going to read out a number of statements which may
apply to policy and practice within your company.
Could you indicate the extent to which each statement applies
to your company using a five-point scale where 5 means that it
is very appropriate and 1 that it is not at all appropriate.

The company practice is:	Very appropriate			Not at all appropriate		Not applic-able	Don't know
To expect loyalty from employees in return for an advanced welfare package	5	4	3	2	1	0	X

To encourage all employees to fulfil their maximum potential	5	4	3	2	1	0	X
To consider that the company's obligations to the workforce are confined only to working hours	5	4	3	2	1	0	X
To *inform* employees or their representatives on a regular basis about company objectives and day-to-day management	5	4	3	2	1	0	X
To accept that most employees are committed to their unions and hence to encourage collective bargaining on a regular basis	5	4	3	2	1	0	X
To *involve* employees in full partnership with management to serve the overall objectives of the company as a whole	5	4	3	2	1	0	X

77 Thinking now about your company's policy on pay, how would you position the company on a five-point scale where 5 represents a company which believes in providing employees with an above-average pay and welfare package, and 1 represents a company which feels it has to keep labour costs as low as possible?

Above average pay and welfare 5

4

3

2

Labour costs as low as possible 1
Don't know X

78 What incentive payment schemes, if any, do you have (apart from those already discussed)?

```
Payment by results ........................  1
Individual bonus schemes, for example, measured
    day work .............................  2
Plant-wide bonus schemes .................  3
Commission ...............................  4
Other (WRITE IN) _____
          _____  V
```

79a Can I just check: what is the *main* business activity of _____
(ENTERPRISE NAME)?

_____
_____
_____

79b And what other business activities is _____
(ENTERPRISE NAME) involved in?

_____
_____
_____

80 Is _____(ENTERPRISE NAME) UK owned or foreign
owned?
```
UK owned/controlled ......................  1
50/50 UK and foreign ownership ...........  2
Foreign owned/controlled .................  3
```

81a Does _____ (ENTERPRISE NAME) consist of a number of
different establishments or a single independent establishment?
```
No. of different establishments ..........  1
```
Approximately how many?
```
Single independent establishment .........  2
```

81b How much autonomy does each establishment have? I am
thinking particularly with regard to the introduction of profit-
sharing/share-ownership schemes?
```
No autonomy/all decisions centralized, taken
    at HQ ................................  1
Some autonomy – for example, can initiate schemes
    but have to submit for approval ......  2
Complete autonomy – for example, no authorization
    needed from HQ .......................  3
```

82 Has your organization's workforce increased, decreased, or
stayed the same over the last five years?
```
Increased ....................  1
Decreased ....................  2
Stayed the same ..............  3
```

143

83 And what about the trend in business volume over the same
period?

Increased 1
Decreased 2
Stayed the same 3

84 Finally, what are the approximate capital assets of _____
(ENTERPRISE NAME)?

_____

85 And into which of these ranges does the organization's
annual turnover in the last financial year fall?

Under £1m 1   £100–£199m 6
£1m–under £3½m 2   £200–£499m 7
£3½–£10m 3   £500–£999m 8
£11–£49m 4   £1000m or more 9
£50–£99m 5

THANK YOU VERY MUCH FOR YOUR TIME AND HELP
WITH THIS SURVEY.

Telephone interviews: firms with no generally based schemes

PROFIT-SHARING AND SHARE-OWNERSHIP SCHEMES
TELEPHONE INTERVIEW (2)
(i.e. with those who have no generally based schemes)

1a Has _____ (ENTERPRISE NAME) ever operated a
profit-sharing or share-ownership scheme *applying to all or
most employees?*

Yes ... 1
No ... 2

1b   i) Was it:

An Inland Revenue-approved profit-sharing
scheme 1
SAYE share-option scheme 2
Other share-ownership scheme 3
Cash-based profit-sharing scheme 4
Other (WRITE IN) _____

_____ V

ii) Did it apply to:

or   Your whole company in the UK 1
To certain divisions only 2

iii) Did it cover:

Full-time staff only 1
Both full- and part-time staff 2

iv) What was the necessary period of service?

```
6 years + ................................. 6
5 years ................................... 5
4 years ................................... 4
3 years ................................... 3
2 years ................................... 2
1 year or less ............................. 1
None .................................... 0
```

v) When was the scheme discontinued?

Year ⬜

vi) Why was it discontinued?

_____
_____
_____

2a Have you considered or are you considering the introduction of a scheme applying to all or most employees?

```
Considering  ...................... 1
Have considered but rejected  ........ 2

Not considered .................... 3
```

2b What types of scheme did you consider?

```
Inland Revenue-approved profit sharing ....... 1
SAYE ................................... 2
Other (WRITE IN) _____
_____ V
```

2c Why was the idea rejected?

```
Too costly in administration  ................. 1
Too costly, that is, too much money going out to
    employees  ........................... 2
Restructuring of company  .................. 3
Change of management  .................... 4
Other (WRITE IN) _____
_____ V
```

ASK IF CONSIDERING SCHEME (CODE 1 A Q2a)

3a What stage have you reached in your considerations?
       Still a vague plan 1
       Looking into different schemes 2
       Chosen a scheme 3
       Waiting for approval 4
       Received approval, about to put into operation . 5
       Other (WRITE IN) _____
       _____ V

3b What type of scheme will it be?
       Inland Revenue-approved profit sharing 1
       SAYE 2
       Other share ownership 3
              shares 4
       Other profit sharing
              cash 5
       Other (WRITE IN) _____
       _____ V

3c Will it apply to:
       Your whole company in the UK 1
       Certain divisions 2

3d How many staff (approximately) will be eligible?

                                                         _____

3e What level of participation do you expect?

                       [   ] %
                    Don't know . . . .

4   Why did you choose this type of scheme?
    PROBE: What are its advantages over other types of schemes?
    _____
    _____
    _____

ASK CONSIDERERS, OTHERS GO TO Q5b

5a I am going to read out a number of objectives which companies
    may hope to achieve by introducing a profit-sharing or share-
    ownership scheme. Can you indicate how important each one
    is in your case on a scale of 1 to 5, where 5 is 'very important'
    and 1 is 'not at all important'?

ASK NON-CONSIDERERS

5b I am going to read out a number of possible benefits which can result from introducing a profit-sharing or share-ownership scheme. Can you indicate how important each of these could be to you, using a scale of 1 to 5, where 5 is 'very important' and 1 is 'not at all important'?

5c		Very important				Not at all important	Don't know
A	To make employees more profit conscious/more interested in the company's success	5	4	3	2	1	X
B	To increase employees' sense of commitment to the company/make staff more likely to stay	5	4	3	2	1	X
C	To act as an incentive for greater productivity	5	4	3	2	1	X
D	To make employees feel that they are part of the company – working *with* it, not just *for* it	5	4	3	2	1	X
E	To help hold wage claims down	5	4	3	2	1	X
F	To provide tax-efficient means of reward:						
	i) for the employees	5	4	3	2	1	X
	ii) for the company	5	4	3	2	1	X
G	To ensure that employees benefit from the company's profitability	5	4	3	2	1	X
H	To increase employees' understanding of the financial issues that face the company	5	4	3	2	1	X
I	To increase the sense of co-operation between management and workforce	5	4	3	2	1	X

The origins of economic democracy

ASK NON-CONSIDERERS

6a What would you say are the *main* factors which prevent you from introducing:
i) a profit-sharing scheme for all employees?

_____
_____
_____
_____

ii) a share-ownership scheme for all employees?

_____
_____
_____
_____

6b Is this situation/attitude likely to change over the next few years?

Yes 1
No 2

6c In what way?

_____
_____
_____
_____

148

References

Abell, P. (1985) 'Industrial democracy, has it a future? The West European experience', *Journal of General Management* 10: 50–62.

Bell, D. (1973) *The Coming of Post-Industrial Society*, New York: Basic Books.

Beloff, M. (1948) *Thomas Jefferson and American Democracy*, London: Hutchinson.

Blanchflower, D. G. and Oswald, A. J. (1987) 'Profit sharing – can it work?', *Oxford Economic Papers* 39: 1–19.

Brannen, P. (1983) *Authority and Participation in Industry*, London: Batsford.

Bristow, E. (1974) 'Profit-sharing, socialism and labour unrest', in K. D. Brown (ed.) *Essays in Anti-Labour History*, London: Macmillan, pp. 262–89.

Brown, W. (ed.) (1981) *The Changing Contours of British Industrial Relations*, Oxford: Blackwell.

Brown, W. and Sisson, K. (1984) 'Current trends and future possibilities', in M. J. F. Poole, W. Brown, J. Rubery, K. Sisson, R. Tarling, and F. Wilkinson (eds) *Industrial Relations in the Future*, London: Routledge & Kegan Paul, pp. 11–38.

Church, R. A. (1971) 'Profit sharing and labour relations in England in the nineteenth century', *International Review of Social History* 14: 2–16.

Clegg, H. A. (1976) *Trade Unionism Under Collective Bargaining*, Oxford: Blackwell.

Copeman, G. (1958) *The Challenge of Employee Shareholding*, London: Business Publications.

Copeman, G., Moore, P., and Arrowsmith, C. (1984) *Shared Ownership*, Aldershot: Gower.

Cronin, J. E. (1979) *Industrial Conflict in Modern Britain*, London: Croom Helm.

Daniel, W. and Millward, N. (1983) *Workplace Industrial Relations in Britain*, London: Heinemann.

Deloitte, Haskins, and Sells (1985) *Finance Bill 1985*, London: Deloitte, Haskins, and Sells.

Doeringer, P. B. and Piore, M. J. (1971) *Internal Labor Markets and Manpower Analysis*, Lexington, MA: Heath.

149

The origins of economic democracy

Edwards, P. K. (1986) *Conflict at Work*, Oxford: Blackwell.
Flanders, A. (1970) *Management and Unions*, London: Faber & Faber.
Gallie, D. (1978) *In Search of the New Working Class*, Cambridge: Cambridge University Press.
Gordon, R., Edwards, R., and Reich, M. (1982) *Labour Market Segmentation in American Capitalism*, Cambridge: Cambridge University Press.
Gurdon, M. A. (1985) 'Equity participation by employees: the growing debate in West Germany', *Industrial Relations* 24: 113–29.
Guski, H. G. and Schneider, J. H. (1977) *Betriebliche Vermogensbeteiligung in der Bundersrepublic Deutchland*, Koln: Deutscher Instituts-Verlag.
Hammer, T. (1985) 'The history of the Rath buyout: a role expectation analysis', paper presented to the Industrial Relations Research Association, December.
Hammer, T. and Strauss, G. (1986) *Workers' Participation in the US*, Mimeo.
Income Data Services (1987) *Report No. 496*, p. 29.
Industrial Democracy in Europe International Research Group (IDE) (1979) 'Participation: formal rules, influence and involvement', *Industrial Relations* 18: 273–94.
Industrial Democracy in Europe International Research Group (IDE) (1981a) *European Industrial Relations*, Oxford: Clarendon Press.
Industrial Democracy in Europe International Research Group (IDE) (1981b) *Industrial Democracy in Europe*, Oxford: Clarendon Press.
Industrial Participation (1985–6) *Report No. 589*, pp. 17–25.
Ingham, G. K. (1974) *Strikes and Industrial Conflict*, London: Macmillan.
Jones, G. P. and Pool, A. G. (1940) *A Hundred Years of Economic Development*, London: Duckworth.
Kerr, C. (1983) *The Future of Industrial Societies*, Cambridge, MA: Harvard University Press.
Kerr, C., Dunlop, J. T., Harbison, F., and Myers, C. A. (1960) *Industrialism and Industrial Man*, Cambridge, MA: Harvard University Press.
Kilmann, R. (1986) *Beyond the Quick Fix*, San Francisco: Jossey–Bass.
Klein, K. J. and Rosen, C. (1986) 'Employee stock ownership in the United States', in R. Stern and S. McCarthy (eds) *International Yearbook of Organizational Democracy*, vol. 3, Chichester: Wiley, pp. 387–406.
Kumar, K. (1978) *Prophecy and Progress*, Harmondsworth: Penguin.
Marx, K. (1858) *Grundrisse*, transl. by M. Nicholaus (Harmondsworth: Penguin, 1973).
Matthews, D. (1988) 'The British experience of profit-sharing: 1880–1980', *Economic History Review*, in press.
Melling, J. (1983) 'Employers, industrial welfare, and the struggle for workplace control in British industry, 1880–1920', in H. F. Gospel and C. R. Littler (eds) *Managerial Strategies and Industrial Relations*, London: Heinemann, pp. 55–81.

150

Mill, J. S. (1965) *Collected Works*, J. M. Robson (ed.), Toronto and London: University of Toronto Press.

Millward, N. and Stevens, M. (1986) *British Workplace Industrial Relations 1980–1984*, Aldershot: Gower.

Pateman, C. (1968) *Participation and Democratic Theory*, Cambridge: Cambridge University Press.

Phelps Brown, E. H. (1960) *The Growth of British Industrial Relations*, London: Macmillan.

Poole, M. J. F. (1982) 'Theories of industrial democracy: the emerging synthesis', *Sociological Review* 30: 181–207.

Poole, M. J. F. (1984) 'A framework for analysis and an appraisal of main developments', in M. J. F. Poole, W. Brown, J. Rubery, K. Sisson, R. Tarling, and F. Wilkinson (eds) *Industrial Relations in the Future*, London: Routledge & Kegan Paul, pp. 39–94.

Poole, M. J. F. (1986a) *Industrial Relations: Origins and Patterns of National Diversity*, London: Routledge & Kegan Paul.

Poole, M. J. F. (1986b) *Towards a New Industrial Democracy*, London: Routledge & Kegan Paul.

Poole, M. J. F., Mansfield, R., Blyton, P. R., and Frost, P. E. (1982) 'Managerial attitudes and behaviour in industrial relations: evidence from a national survey', *British Journal of Industrial Relations* 14: 339–55.

Purcell, J. and Sisson, K. (1983) 'Strategies and practice in the management of industrial relations', in G. S. Bain (ed.) *Industrial Relations in Britain*, Oxford: Blackwell, pp. 95–120.

Ramsay, H. (1977) 'Cycles of control', *Sociology* 11: 481–506.

Ramsay, H. (1983) 'Evolution or cycle? Worker participation in the 1970s and 1980s', in C. Crouch and F. A. Heller (eds) *International Yearbook of Organizational Democracy*, vol. 1, Chichester: Wiley, pp. 203–25.

Ramsay, H. and Haworth, N. (1984) 'Worker capitalists? Profit-sharing, capital-sharing and juridical forms of socialism', *Economic and Industrial Democracy* 5: 295–324.

Rosen, C. M., Klein, K. J., and Young, K. M. (1986) *Employee Ownership in America*, Lexington, MA: Lexington Books.

Rousseau, J. J. (1968) *The Social Contract*, transl. by M. Cranston, Harmondsworth: Penguin.

Rubery, J., Tarling, R., and Wilkinson, F. (1984) 'Industrial relations issues in the 1980s: an economic analysis', in M. J. F. Poole, W. Brown, J. Rubery, K. Sisson, R. Tarling, and F. Wilkinson (eds) *Industrial Relations in the Future*, London: Routledge & Kegan Paul, pp. 95–137.

Smith, G. R. (1986) 'Profit sharing and share ownership in Britain', *Employment Gazette* 94: 380–5.

Stern, R. N. and McCarthy, S. (eds) (1986) *International Yearbook of Organizational Democracy*, vol. 3, Chichester: Wiley.

Tannenbaum, A., Cook, H., and Lochmann, J. (1984) 'The relationship of employee ownership to the technological adaptiveness and performance of companies', unpublished paper, Ann Arbor, MI: Institute for Social Research.

151

Thurley, K. E. and Wood, S. J. (1983) 'Business strategy and industrial relations strategy', in K. E. Thurley and S. J. Wood (eds) *Industrial Relations and Management Strategy*, Cambridge: Cambridge University Press, pp. 197–224.

Webb, S. and Webb, B. (1897) *Industrial Democracy*, London: Longman.

Webb, S. and Webb, B. (1914) 'Cooperative production and profit sharing', *New Statesman*, 45, 14 February, suppl.

Webb, S. and Webb, B. (1920) *Industrial Democracy*, London: Longman.

Whyte, W. F., Hammer, T., Meek, C., Nelson, R., and Stern, R. (1983) *Worker Participation in Ownership*, Ithaca, NY: Institute of Labor Relations Press.

Woodworth, W. P. (1981) 'Towards a labor-owned economy in the United States', *Labour and Society* 6: 41–56.

Index

153

against takeovers, 71–2; and staff
retention, 70; and timing of
introduction of schemes, 72–4
manufacturing, 32–3
Marx, K., 9
materialist theories, 53; *see also*
structuralist models
Matthews, D., 11, 12
mechanistic authoritarian
organizations, 36
Melling, J., 9, 10
Mill, J. S., 4
Millward, N., 44, 45
Ministry of Labour, 13
models of profit-sharing and share-
ownership schemes, 26–7, 53,
105–6; *see also* explanatory
frameworks of profit sharing and
share ownership
moral commitment, 70
Morris, 12

Needlers, 12
Netherlands, the, 15, 17
New England, 19
new technology, 33
New Zealand, 15, 17
non-approved schemes, 47–9, 125
Norway, 15, 17

organizational democracy, theory
of, 2–8, 104–5
Oswald, A. J., 44

Pateman, C., 4
paternal 'styles', 34, 35
pay policy, 90–2
payment systems, 90–2, 111
payroll tax, 23
personnel departments, 72
Phelps Brown, E. H., 9
'philanthropic' outlook, 9
Piore, M. J., 31
Pool, A. G., 12
Poole, M. J. F., 2, 7, 33, 34, 37,
41
Portugal, 15, 17
post-industrial society, the, 32

private companies, profit sharing
and share ownership in, 46–7, 49
professional managers, 30
Profit-sharing and employee-
shareholding schemes, 1–24,
25–37, 38–52, 53–66, 67–92,
93–102, 103–113; and collective
representation, 93–102;
developments in Britain, 8–14;
and economic 'infrastructure',
53–66; explanatory frameworks
of, 25–37; government role in
development of, 28–52; and
industrial relations climate,
81–92; international
developments in, 14–24; and
managerial strategies and
'styles', 67–80; and theories of
developments in, 2–8
protection against takeover, 71–2
publicly-quoted companies, 29–30,
46–7, 49
Purcell, J., 34, 35
pure economic democracy, 3

Ramsay, H., 2, 5, 10, 12, 13, 24
Rath Meat Packing Company, 19
Regional Councils, 23
regression analysis, 114–15
respondent identification, 123
response rates, 122
'revolution from the top', 22
Rosen, C. M., 19, 21, 41
Rousseau, J. J., 4
Rubery, J., 31

sample characteristics, 122
Schneider, J. H., 22
segmentation of labour, 31–2
self-management, 3
services, 32–3
shareholding *see* profit-sharing and
employee-shareholding schemes
Silicon Valley-type companies, 33
Singapore, 15, 17
size of enterprise, 30–1
'smoke stack industries', 19
Social Democratic Party, the, 23

Printed in the United States
by Baker & Taylor Publisher Services